Precarious Rhapsody

Semiocapitalism and the pathologies of the post-alpha generation

Franco "Bifo" Berardi

<.:.Min0r.:.>
.c0mp0siti0ns.

Precarious Rhapsody
Semiocapitalism and the pathologies of the post-alpha generation

Franco "Bifo" Berardi

ISBN 978-1-57027-207-3

Edited by Erik Empson & Stevphen Shukaitis
Translated by Arianna Bove, Melinda Cooper, Erik Empson, Michael
Goddard, Giuseppina Mecchia, Antonella Schintu, Tiziana Terranova,
and Steve Wright

Bifo extends special thanks to Arianna, Erik and Stevphen for making
this publication possible. Thanks to the 1750 subscribers of the netzine
(www.rekombinant.org) who have been reading my postings during the
last eight years, and have helped in creating a large deterritorialized community of free thinkers.

Released by Minor Compositions
Wivenhoe / New York / Port Watson

Minor Compositions is a series of interventions & provocations drawing from autonomous politics, avant-garde aesthetics, and the revolutions of everyday life.

Minor Compositions is an imprint of Autonomedia
www.minorcompositions.info | minorcompositions@gmail.com

Distributed by Autonomedia
PO Box 568 Williamsburgh Station
Brooklyn, New York 11211-0568 USA

Table of Contents

altraverso

numero ultimo
sett. 1977 L.250

Le facce cattive/PUNK/ mentre i nostri buoni/ indiani boyscouts/
te be happy together donne chiappe tenerezza/ monstre/ ed anche
i nostri cattivi/ sono cattivi però/
solo
a fin di bene.
ORA/ senza chiedere/ sentiamo con le antenne/ che han percepito crescere
sotto la dura corazza/ della politica un flusso/ de tendresse/
Now/stracciamo questo foglio/ che abbiamo scritto, mappa/ chiara e
limpide per/ chi voleva trovare/ il tesoro/ e/ AVVERTIAMO (nel senso
di: percepismo)/ il passo duro dei nomadi/ del lavoro a/traverso/
frontiere/ che cercano di trattenerli/ con panoplie de mesures/
pour lutter contre le faux malades/ con SuperPhenix spettrale/
ARBEITSMARKET/ in giganteschi Gulag disseminati/ e i bravi/ ragazzi
(della Città futura)/ che telefonano subito/ in Questura.

Terremo il passo.
Rompendo
le fila.
A/traverso

Le préfet Jannin félicite les forces de l'ordre
pour «leur tenue face
aux gauchistes et aux étrangers»

si scioglie (ma quando mai fu

solido)?
Per rompere. E come quando
dirigeva (lui)

H ELMUT SCHMIDT

L'an un de la gauche

Egli era un uomo usano per ogni vana
Verso un unico obiettivo,era
dirigermi invece verso cento obiettivi

diversi, non
è vero che esiste

Decision Time

Les vieux démons

Zeit

una società (quale?)se ciascuna tensione
chiare fresche dolci acque
costituisce un flusso
che oggi è possibile
il comaniamo come
insurrezione involontaria in cui

Arbeitsmarkt: Der Konsens ist d...ll

i flussi si compongono
E' possibile, basta
rompere questo involucre,il limite.

"God is dead, Marx is dead, and I'm not feeling too well myself"

Le rapport secret de l'absentéisme
Schleyer une panoplie de mesures répres...
pour lutter contre les faux malades

Lo diciamo. Spezzare
la barriera del tempo
di lavoro per cogliere
l'attività. Passione.

il culo insanguinato di Queen Elisabeth rosa

confetto con Amendola

l'annuncia.A Schleyer strappati gli occhi

Vogliono occ

upare B

Per i padroni è finita.
Non un'altra società, ma la fine
di ogni unità terribile. In più lingue
la vita.

ologna

HYSTOERIE

**PER LA CRITICA DELLA
RIVOLUZIONE**
FARE LA RIVOLUZIONE

0. Bifurcations

Introduction

An infinite series of bifurcations: this is how we can tell the story of our life, of our loves, but also the history of revolts, defeats and restorations of order. At any given moment different paths open up in front of us, and we are continually presented with the alternative of going here or going there. Then we decide, we cut out from a set of infinite possibilities and choose a single path. But do we really choose? Is it really a question of a choice, when we go here rather than there? Is it really a choice, when masses go to shopping centers, when revolutions are transformed into massacres, when nations enter into war? It is not we who decide but the concatenations: machines for the liberation of desires and mechanisms of control over the imaginary. The fundamental bifurcation is always this one: between machines for liberating desire and mechanisms of control over the imaginary. In our time of digital mutation, technical automatisms are taking control of the social psyche.

Pathogenic fluxes of dependency enervate the collective imaginary, forcing the desiring body into submission. The more the network of possibilities thickens, thanks to globalization, network technologies and social and territorial mobility, the more we find ourselves trapped by the automatisms that rule individual choices: technological, financial and psychic automatisms transform the multitude into a swarm.

It would be possible to recount the history of the twentieth century from the point of view of its bifurcations. The bifurcations between utopian imaginings and real dystopia are continually represented in the histories of artistic avant-gardes and revolutionary movements. The de-structuring passion of Italian Futurism placed itself in the service of publicity, the mechanism of control over the collective imaginary. The creative joyfulness of Russian Futurism placed itself in the service of Bolshevik terror. Surrealism fed the engineering of the imagination. Egalitarian revolt transformed itself into state dictatorships. The creative movements furnished semio-capitalism with labor power.

In the last few years I have sought to reconstruct the labyrinth of utopian bifurcations that followed the creative explosion of 1968, up until the key moment of 1977 when all the utopias of the twentieth century were converted into their opposite. Beginning from the reconstruction of this labyrinth, I have attempted to interrogate the present bifurcations, the bifurcations that open up continuously in the proliferation of possibilities. In this book, I have gathered together the traces of this work. They are perhaps still confused, the way traces are. Written in the years that followed the revolt of Seattle, the first act of conscious, mass self-organization of cognitive labor, they cross diverse disciplinary fields, from sociocultural analysis to psychopathology, to the sociology of communication, to political theory.

The first part is dedicated to the year of premonitions, to the 1977 of Italian autonomies and free radios that was also the year of Sid Vicious' *No Future*, the year of Schleyer's homicide and the tragedy of Stammheim. *"When the Future Began"* reconstructs the bifurcations that presented themselves before the movements when, in September of that year, one hundred thousand people convened in Bologna to interrogate the future without finding any answer. The movements didn't choose but followed the traces that the ideological vision inscribed on their neurons had superimposed over reality: armed violence, heroin and mass contrition.

The second part is dedicated to the social and productive transformation of the last thirty years: from worker revolt against the assembly line, to post-industrial technical restructuring, to the emergence of the cognitariat, the virtual unorganizable class of mental labor. Here, the sage, the merchant and the warrior confront each other on the stage of late twentieth century history. Scientific and artistic creativity are captured by the market and by war. This leads to the question of how is it possible to reconstruct autonomy within the conditions of semio-capital.

The third part analyses the formation process of the networked infosphere: the mutation that follows the diffusion of digital media technologies, the construction of systems for the pervasion of the collective mind on the part of the techno-sphere and the emergence of a mass media competency that led to the formation of a media-active movement.

The fourth part revolves around the psycho-sphere, the sensibility of the first media generations: the video-electronic generation, the one that was born after the advent of color TV, those born at the end of the 1970s or in the first years of the 1980s. And above all it concerns the connective generation, the one which was born in the 1990s that grew up in symbiosis with a network of virtual innervations: imaginary, psychic and bionic prostheses.

The fifth part goes to the heart of the spreading psychopathology of the generations that have learnt more words from a machine than from their mother, as the anthropologist Rose Golden wrote in 1975. The argument concerns the disappearance of the mother and the consequent break between the learning of language and affectivity.

The perspective that emerges from these chapters has the character of a catastrophe of modern humanism, but every situation of catastrophe opens onto a bifurcation. It can collapse in an infernal spiral if it remains hostage to the dominant economic dogmas and continues on the road leading to an augmentation of forces in the wrong direction. Or an epistemological rupture can be confirmed, a post-economic paradigm can emerge and an entirely new vision be revealed of relations between human beings. The subject of this rupture can only be cognitive labor. Only the autonomy of mental labor from economic rule can deactivate the suicidal mechanism of war and the obsession with growth that devastates the planet. Cognitive, networked, precarious labor is the transversal function capable of recombining the social elements in perennial mutation according to a non-accumulative, non-competitive and non-aggressive principle.

But the increasing autonomy of the transversal cognitive function cannot achieve this before the trauma will have produced its effects. And these effects could be irreversible.

The end of modern politics

The parties of the left which, in the course of the twentieth century, have betrayed and dispersed the ideals and expectations of the working class in order to avoid disappearing altogether, are today desperately seeking to pick up the same thread with the new generations. But the heirs of Leninism and social democracy are no longer capable of interpreting the signs that come from the new social reality, and oscillate between a 'reformist' position of subordination to liberal hyper-capitalism and a 'resistant' position that re-proposes old ideologies in a defensive and residual form.

Participation in political life has appeared to progressively diminish and there does not seem to be any remedy for this disaffection. The populations of Western countries do not renounce the exercise of the electoral right to vote. But voting is an ever decreasing sign of true political participation, because everyone realizes that rather than being able to decide between real alternatives, they are only able to pick the faces and names of those who will impose pre-packaged and inevitable decisions upon them.

Since the time in 1981 when François Mitterand, six months after being elected President of the French Republic, abandoned the socialist program which had been presented to voters, recognizing in an explicit way the impossibility of governing without following the rules imposed by large economic forces, it has been evident that right and left are two words deprived of substantial signification. If political discourse has any sense, it indicates the ability of associated human beings to choose between alternatives. Inasmuch as these alternatives no longer exist because automatisms prevail, at this point politics no longer exists and political participation becomes a ritual without significance in which citizens participate only through conformism.

The origin of modern politics lies in the cultural perspective inaugurated by humanism, and by the discovery of the dimension that is free will. In the *Discourse on Human Dignity* that Pico della Mirandola wrote in the last decade of the fifteenth century, human potential is not limited by any archetype, norm or necessity, because the creator has not determined in any way the route that human power should follow:

> I have given you, Adam, neither a determined role, nor your own appearance, nor any prerogative of your own, because this role, this appearance, this prerogative is what you will desire precisely, according to your vow and your counsel, achievements and preserves. The determined nature of the other beings is contained within the norms prescribed by me. You will determine your nature yourself, with no imposed barrier, according to your own will, the power of which will advise you. You are placed in the middle of the world, because from there you can better distinguish all that there is in the world. I have made you neither celestial nor terrestrial, neither mortal nor immortal, because you yourself, as a free and sovereign artisan, will shape and sculpt yourself in the form that you will have pre-selected. You could degenerate into something inferior, as are the brutes; you could

regenerate yourself, according to your will, into something superior, as are the divine. In nascent man, the Lord put the seeds
of every species and the germs of every life (Pico della Mirandola, *Discourse on Human Dignity*)

The day in which God created man, according to Pico, he had fin-
ished with the archetypes at his disposition, and his favorite creature, the
last and the most complex, could neither be defined by any archetype
nor any essence. God must therefore leave to man the freedom to define
himself, to freely establish the limits of his actions and the lines of his
destiny. Human becoming was neither delimited nor finalized by divine
will, but was consigned to the free will of man. Modernity inaugurates
itself under the sign of this awareness: man is a project, not the development and realization of an implicit design in the divine will or in the folds
of Being. Within this void of Being the story of modernity unfolds. Heidegger says:

> As ek-sisting, man sustains Da-sein in that he takes the *Da*, the
> clearing of being, into "care." But Da-sein itself occurs essentially
> as "thrown." It unfolds essentially in the throw of Being as the
> fateful sending (1993: 231).

In the difference of beings with respect to Being, lies the excess and
the singularity of being-there (Da-sein), of being in a situation. But the
technical development of human intelligence prepares the end of human
freedom as founded on indetermination. Human freedom has constructed, in the course of the modern age, a fate that objectifies itself in
technology up until the point it has penetrated language, enfolding it in
its automatisms. Thanks to technics, the will to power has produced the
instruments for its own end and the end of human freedom, and so of the
human itself, inasmuch as the human is that freedom that technology
cancels.

But there is an even more radical and insurmountable reason for
which the political message of modernity cannot be translated into the
language of the latest generations, the video-electronic generation, born
at the end of the 1970s, and the connective generation born in the first
years of the 1990s. Intergenerational transmission has become impossible
because of a problem of cognitive formats and not only due to a problem
of contents. The mind of the generation which was formed within the

technical conditions of video-electronics, and then that which is being formed internally to the connective conditions of the net, functions in a manner that is increasingly incompatible with the alphabetic, critical, historical mind, that is to say the mind of modern humanity, the one that believed in the political possibility of choosing between alternatives.

I have always found the concept of generation suspect. In the past industrial era, the concept of social class defined processes of identification and conflicts much better. Social classes do not coincide completely with generations, because the formation lines of social class consciousness pass through processes of production and distribution of income, rather than through generational memberships. In the industrial era, generational succession had a marginal importance and could neither determine effects of radical differentiation, nor could it influence politically significant forms of consciousness and identification. As long as political subjectivity was formed internally to the social division of labor, generational subjectivity was only a socio-biological concept, unsuitable for defining the historical characteristics of subjective consciousness.

But the post-industrial transformation has confused the terms of the problem. On an objective level, social and economic stratifications have certainly not been lessened, but this no longer seems in a position to produce decisive effects of identification on the level of consciousness. The fragmentation and increasing precariousness of productive processes has rendered social identity extremely fragile, at the same time as identity is made ever more imaginary and consciousness vectoral. In postmodern processes of identification, what we are is less important than what we could be, and today the formation of subjectivity passes through a differential branding of a generational type, that is much more significant than it was in the past.

With the concept of generations we are making reference to a human togetherness that shares a temporally defined technological, cognitive and imaginary formative environment. In the past era of modernity this formative environment changed slowly over time, while productive and economic relations and the relationships between social classes changed in a much more pronounced way. But once alphabetic technologies gave way to digitalization, this transformation has intervened to radically modify the modalities of learning, memorization and linguistic exchange, and the formative density of generational belonging has become decisive.

At this point we no longer identify the concept of generations with simply a biological phenomenon, but rather a technological and cognitive phenomenon, the trans-subjective self-constitution of a common horizon of conscious and experiential possibility. The transformation of the techno-cognitive environment redefines the possibilities and limits of individuation.

Because of this, I believe that it is necessary to identify the new forms of social consciousness beginning from generational belonging. And for this reason I will speak of two decisive successive shifts in a mutation that has led to the draining of humanistic categories and of the perspectives on which modern politics was based. These two passages are constituted in the subsumption of the human mind in formation within two successive technological configurations of the media-sphere. The first is that which I call video-electronic, meaning the technologies of televisual communication. It is a case of the passage that Marshall McLuhan speaks of in his fundamental 1964 study, *Understanding Media*.

McLuhan looks at the transition from the alphabetic sphere to the video-electronic one and concludes that when the simultaneous succeeds the sequential, the capacity of mythological elaboration succeeds that of critical elaboration. The critical faculty presupposes a particular structuring of the message: the sequentiality of writing, the slowness of reading, and the possibility of judging in sequence the truth or falsity of statements. It is in these conditions that the critical discrimination that has characterized the cultural forms of modernity becomes possible. But in the sphere of video-electronic communication, critique becomes progressively substituted by a form of mythological thinking in which the capacity to distinguish between the truth and falsity of statements becomes not only irrelevant but impossible. This passage took place in the techno-sphere and media-sphere of the 1960s and 1970s and the generation that was born at the end of the 1970s began to manifest the first signs of impermeability to the values of politics and critique that had been fundamental for the preceding generations of the twentieth century.

The more radical mutation was the diffusion of digital technologies and the formation of the global internet during the 1990s. Here, the functional modality of the human mind changes completely, not only because the conditions of communication become infinitely more complex, saturated and accelerated, but rather because the infantile mind begins to form itself in a media environment completely different from that of modern humanity.

The studies that I have collected in the section concerning the psycho-sphere are dedicated to this connective generation.

First bifurcation: 77 the year of premonition

When the future began

What happened in Italy in 1977 is difficult to understand in the framework of modern political concepts. At the time, Italy was in a deeply conflictual period, and a strong movement of students and young proletarians had surfaced, challenging economic and state power.

The year 1977 is generally recorded as a year of violence. Indeed it was the year that the Red Brigades started their crazy, bloody campaigns, and the riots that exploded in the streets of Rome, Bologna and many other towns at the time were not at all peaceful meetings and friendly promenades. But violence was not an issue when the movement broke out. It became an issue when the police reacted violently to the demonstrations, when the government ordered their repression and the police shot dead students in Bologna and in Rome, and elsewhere.

There was a rage in the air. This was not only because 15% of the population, especially young people, was unemployed. There was a kind of existential rage, a wave of insubordination that was not confined to Italy.

Rather than focus on the violent side of 1977, I prefer to concentrate on the heterogeneous faces of the cultural process which emerged when baby boomers all over the world were hit by the premonition that the modern horizon was drawing to its dissolution.

I want to talk about the general landscape of the 1970s, and it is here that I want to situate the Italian uprising. 1977 is not an Italian year: it is the year when Steve Wozniak and Steven Jobs created the trademark of Apple and what is more, created the tools for spreading information technology; when Alain Minc and Simon Nora wrote *L'informatisation de la société*, a text which theorizes the coming dissolution of nation states due to the political effects of emerging telematics.

In that year Yuri Andropov, secretary of the KGB, wrote a letter to Leonid Brezhnev, arguing that the Soviet Union was in danger of disappearance if the gap with the USA in the field of informatics was not bridged. It was the year when Jean François Lyotard wrote the book *La condition postmoderne*. The year when Charlie Chaplin died; the man with the bowler hat and the cane passed away. This was the year of the end of the twentieth century: the turning point of modernity.

What is special about the Italian situation is not the smoke of the riots and molotov cocktails. In that experience you can see both faces of the changing times: the happy utopian side of creativity and the despair and hopelessness, and terror.

1977 saw the last revolt of the communist proletarians of the twentieth century against capitalist rule and against the bourgeois state. But at the same time it saw the first revolt of the cognitariat, the intellectual workers, and of Technische Wissenschaft Intelligenz.

In the culture produced during that year, we can see the premonition of a new cultural process and a new social landscape. In a rhetorical way, I could call it the first rebellion of the new times that we are living now. But I cannot be sure of this, I do not know if the time we are living now will be again a time of insurrection. Maybe yes, maybe not.

In a certain sense it could be said that we are witnessing the realization of a bad dream, of the dystopian imagination that was present in the movement that exploded in 1977. For that movement was not only, as the legend goes, a happy event, the free expression of creativity. Contained within was a perception of a deep social deterritorialization, of an economic change bound to destroy the human landscape of the cities; bound to subjugate every fragment of time.

In the very chronology of that year we can see the happy phase, which began in 1976 rather than in 1977. But in the months after the violent uprisings in Rome and Bologna, March 1977, one can also see a changing perception, the feeling of terror. In that transition there is something that totally escapes the political framework.

In 1977 Ingmar Bergman produced the movie *The Serpent's Egg*, probably not one of the best movies of Bergman, but a very interesting insight in the construction of the totalitarian mind all the same. When I saw it, right at the end of that year, I felt that in that movie something was directly speaking to me, to us.

The Serpent's Egg is a movie about the incubation of Nazism during the years 1923 to 1933. In those years, the egg of the serpent was slowly opening, and giving birth to the monster. In the time that followed the students' uprising of March 1977 we felt something like this. We detected the smell of a new totalitarianism in the making.

During the months of Spring 1977, scores of militants and intellectuals were arrested, the radio stations of the movement were closed by force, and the movement launched an international meeting against the repression which took place in Bologna in September. A hundred thousand people gathered in Bologna, expecting to hear a magic word of liberation but the magic word was not found.

After the September meeting we perceived the defeat of the movement, the spreading of violence, and the growing strength of the Red Brigades who were gaining energy and militants out of the defeat of the movement.

In Germany, Fall 1977 was a very gloomy month. Hans Martin Schleyer, an important corporate man, was kidnapped and killed by the Rote Armee Fraktion, and some days later, Andreas Baader Carl Hans Raspe and Gudrun Ensslin died in their prison cells in Stammheim, possibly killed by the guards.

The impressive movie by Schlöndorff, Fassbinder and others, *Germany in Autumn* tells of the widespread perception of the coming end of social solidarity. In that movie you can perceive the sudden sadness, the fog, and the clouds descending over people's lives, and the prison of Stammheim becomes a kind of metaphor for the everyday jail that social life is becoming.

Revisiting and reassessing that movement may be interesting if within those times you can find the premonition of what is happening nowadays, the premonition of an anthropological mutation that is unfolding in the new century that we inhabit. Moreover, that movement also created some antidotes to today's problems and some possibilities for looking in another direction.

The social conflict and political framework

I am not an historian, so I cannot reconstruct the historical sequence in a precise way, but I will do my best.

If one looks at the social situation in Italy in 1975-76 there was 15% unemployment, mostly among young people. Since 1969 the factories of the northern cities had been ebullient. In Mirafiori, Alfa Romeo, Petrolchimico, the most important strongholds of the working class, young militants organized radical autonomous struggles, often criticizing the unionist agenda and the political agenda of the Italian Communist Party (PCI). The occupation of Fiat Mirafioni in 1973 was probably the most impressive action against capitalist rule in those years. The majority of the workers in the biggest factory in Italy decided to occupy the place during a long confrontation with the owners. Fiat was the center of economic power, and that struggle became the symbol of resistance of people against capitalist rule.

The young people who had been hired in Fiat during the previous years were mostly migrants coming from the south; Fiat hired young men from Calabria, Sicilia, and from Naples. For those young people it was difficult to exchange the sunny coast of southern Italy, the laziness, the sensuousness of life in the Mediterranean villages, with the smoky, foggy, stressful life of the industrial city.

The occupation was a success. The union and the managers were forced to negotiate on the occupiers' terms. After the struggle of March 1973, when the autonomous organization of the workers decided on the occupation of the factory, the directors of FIAT blocked the turnover of the labor force. No more hiring.

That year, Syria and Egypt attacked Israel on the day of Yom Kippur. The effects of the following war were resented all over the world. Oil prices went crazy. The Western economy was hit terribly leading to recession and crisis with unemployment rising everywhere. The Italian government declared that a period of austerity was necessary and that people had to make sacrifices for the sake of the economy, salaries must stay down, and workers must work harder.

Following this, some people in a demonstration in the streets of Bologna launched the cry:

Loro dicono austerity, noi diciamo dissolutezza sfrenatezza festa.
They say 'austerity,' we answer: 'dissolution, licence, feast.'

Un'onda di leggerezza si diffonde.
A wave of lightness and irresponsibility.

We do not want to pay sacrifice to the God Economy. We do not believe in the dogma of productivity. We shan't give our life to the Gross National Product.

Se l'economia è malata che crepi.
If the economy is sick, may it crack.

I happened to be in Turin in 1973. In that year, all over Europe the car manufacturing factories were washed by a wave of social conflicts. In Fiat Torino, Opel of Russelsheim, Volkswagen and Renault of Billan-court, a massive upheaval of young car-making workers stopped the assembly lines and pushed modern industrial capitalism towards its end. In the Mirafiori factory during the days of the occupation, I saw people disguised as *indiani metropolitani* for the first time; young workers, long-haired with a red scarf around their neck, playing drums in the factory shops.

A square filled with thousands of cars prepared for testing – the horns sounding; hundreds of them. Then the crowd of young workers walked out of the factory beating iron drums. This act of refusal of the sadness of the factory is the premise of the explosion of 1977.

This new generation of workers did not have so much to do with the old tradition of the labor parties. Nor anything to do with the socialist ideology of a state-owned system. A massive refusal of the sadness of work was the leading element behind their protest. Those young workers had much more to do with the hippy movement; much more to do with the history of the avant-garde.

Futurism, Surrealism and Dadaism tried to reinvent the process of political organization. Umberto Eco wrote a paper about this subject, with the title *C'è una nuova lingua: l'italo-indiano*, (There is a new language: Italo-Indian) where he emphasized the linguistic dimension of the new revolt. There he says: the people of the new movement are the children who have read the poems of the Futurists, and are using electronic media for the first time. This is creating a sort of mass avant-garde. Thanks to the technology of the mass media, language is becoming the main site of social confrontation. Poetry (the language which creates shared worlds) had entered the sphere of social change.

This was the starting point of the creation of semiocapitalism, the new regime characterized by the fusion of media and capital. In this sphere, poetry meets advertising and scientific thought meets the enterprise.

In the meantime, while Italian society was in the turmoil of conflict and innovation, the political framework was blocked. The Communists and the Christian Democrats, those two churches of sadness were allied in the common goal of containing and repressing the social movement which was exploding everywhere.

Something should be said about the PCI, which has been known for having a different brand of communism. In the 1960s, the Italian Communist Party was widely credited with having some autonomy from the rule of Moscow. And this was partially true. The party refounded by Palmiro Togliatti in the 1940s was something different to the classical Leninist party as far as the problems of internal organization and political power were concerned. But when it comes to the relationship between society and the state, the PCI has always reacted as a Stalinist party: when it came to social autonomy, Stalinism was the only language they knew.

The PCI has been innovative in the domain of political representation, but it has not created a new language in its relationship to society. So when the movement exploded in the factories and in the universities as a radical struggle against work and against the state, the PCI's response was that of a classical Stalinist party, defending the state and endorsing the repression against the movement.

The government in those years was the result of an alliance between the PCI and the Christian Democrats. The policy of historical compromise aimed at avoiding a social confrontation. But the effect of this policy was the conformation of parliament against the movement and against every socially conflictive action.

Therefore, little political mediation of the social conflict existed, because the absolute majority, almost 100% of parliament, was united against society. This explains the political background of the explosion of 1977.

In 1975 this majority passed a law (Legge Reale, named after the deputy who proposed the bill). This law gave the police the right to shoot people who were supposed to pose a threat. The result was the killing of hundreds of young people who were suspected of carrying weapons although actually they often did not.

Here one can see the conditions of the explosion: 15% of unemployment, mostly young people, social conflict spreading everywhere, and a strong government supported by a parliament where the unified political parties passed repressive laws.

But I am also interested in explaining the social and cultural background. The general framework of the social transformation was the relationship between young workers refusing work in the factories, and students, researchers, and intellectual laborers. 'Operai e studenti uniti nella lotta' was not an empty slogan, it was a good picture of the situation marked by the emergence of a movement of mass intellectuality as a social actor.

Hans Jürgen Krahl, one of the leaders of the student movement in Germany, was the author of a text very important to those times: *Thesen Uber Technisch Wissenschaft Intelligenz*. In it Krahl said that the problem of political organization was no longer disconnected from the social machinery (like in the Leninist age), but was rooted in the self-organization of intellectual labor. Cognitive labor was shifting towards the center of the social scene.

If we are able to connect the refusal of work and techno-scientific intelligence we may discover that intellectual labor is not labor but freedom. The application of technology to automation creates the conditions for a reduction of working time. The relationship between students and workers is not based upon ideology, but upon the understanding of a common ground in the field of knowledge, technology, and freedom from labor.

The last insurrection of the twentieth century

In the spring of 1975, we started printing a zine titled *A/traverso*. The new offset machine gave us the possibility of composing the page in a much freer way than the old typographic printing machine. We used the Dadaist technique of the collage, taking characters from the newspapers, cutting out pictures, mixing and sticking them to the page and then photographing and printing it all. The people who wrote in the zine were the same people who launched Radio Alice in February 1976, a group of young proletarian poets: autonomes desirants, *creativi trasversali*, younger brothers of the students with neckties of 1968. Their reading was less tedious than that of their elder brothers. They were not reading so much Marx and Lenin, but William Burroughs and Roland Barthes. In the pages of *A/traverso*, one central concept was repeated in a thousand ways:

Collective happiness is subversion, subversion is collective happiness

When Radio Alice started broadcasting in February 1976 a dozen anarcho-operaists, post-hippy and proto-punks met in a top floor flat on the roof of the old city of Bologna, and emitted ambiguous signals. The excitation was growing. The political context (the historical compromise of the Communists and of the Catholics) was too narrow for the ebullient society. Conflicts were spreading in the factories, in squats and in scattered events of appropriation all over the country.

Il comunismo è libero e felice dieci cento mille radio alice.
Communism is free and happy: ten hundred thousand Radio Alices

Futurism and Dada were the reference points of this new movement which saw a proliferation of new writing and media such as another magazine *Il Corrispondente Operaio (The Workers' Correspondent)*. We aimed to write point-blank at close range – to aim at the roots – with a soundtrack of Giovanna Marini and Jefferson Airplane. We sought to abolish the separation between art and daily life, or indeed to abolish art and daily life itself.

If in the 1920s the avant-garde had been an elite phenomenon, by the 1970s it was becoming a mass experiment in creating a semiotic environment for life. Thanks to the radios, thanks to the autonomous zines spreading all over, a large scale process of mass irony was launched.

Irony meant the suspension of the semantic heaviness of the world. Suspension of the meaning that we give to gestures, to relationships, to the shape of the thing. We saw it as a suspension of the kingdom of necessity and were convinced that power has power as far as those who have no power take power seriously.

Indeed when irony becomes a mass language, power loses ground, authority and strength. This was time of dissidence, of the ironic from the dogmatic, of Maodadaism: dissidence from the fanaticism of politics and the refusal of labor: dissidence from the fanaticism of the economy.

What does it mean to be rich?

The contradiction between young proletarians and old industrial workers became evident in October 1976 during the struggle at Innocenti, a car producing factory of Milan. Young people, freshly hired, did not take to being exploited and organized themselves defensively by absenteeism: collective escape from work. Some had been fired and the strikes followed as a response. But the old workers did not take part in the strikes believing that the young saboteurs had no right to claim their job as they did not like to work. The question of youth was no more a mere socio-cultural problem, it was becoming a factor in the redefinition of the very political framework of the labor movement, and a factor of social recomposition.

Young people were suffering because of the effects of the recession that had begun in 1973 following the oil shock caused by the war of Yom Kippur. Unemployment was high amongst the young, and precarious labor began to spread for the first time. The movement did not fight for full employment but for money. Legal and illegal actions of appropriation and the sharing of goods were spreading. Young people shared everything: houses, clothes, objects for daily life. People were working less and taking more time for pleasure. There was absolutely no feeling of sacrifice, the recession notwithstanding: no poverty, no renunciation. To be rich was not seen as possessing many things to consume, but having time to enjoy. To be rich did not mean having a large amount of money, but enough to live without working too much.

You see what an enigmatic question was posed: why there are periods when human bodies attract each other, and souls pleasantly lie together, and periods when empathy seems to dissolve and human beings stay alone in despair? Which dynamic results in the heavy architectures of depression and which dynamic governs the light architectures of happily living together?

The simultaneous hostility towards the capitalist regime and the PCI led the movement to break all the relationships with the historical left. The fight against the PCI reached its climax in February 1977, when the Communist leader of the unions, Luciano Lama, was expelled from the University of Rome, where he had gone with many bodyguards in order to parade and propagandize the political agenda of the Stalinist-reformist party, which was controlling the government together with the Christian Democrats.

The agenda of the PCI aimed at pitting the workers who have a regular job against the irregular, unemployed, precarious, underpaid young proletarians. Thousands of students, metropolitan Indians and young workers gathered in the big square and make an infernal noise all around. The atmosphere became heated, and the boss forced to leave. The movement refused the distinction of regular workers and the unemployed. "We all are precarious" they shouted. Thirty years later we know how right they were.

The city of Bologna was the symbol of capitalist-communist power. In those years Bologna was a very lively city. The university was filled with students coming from the southern regions of the country, and many others coming from abroad. Teachers of great fame and wisdom were teaching in that period. The new department for arts and music had just opened, and it was an attractor for many students who wanted to mix poetry and political action, social engagement and art.

Bologna is also a very conservative city. This is the region where Fascism had been launched and created, and after the First World War, the social class that gave birth to Fascism, had converted to this special blend of reformist Stalinism that the PCI embodied.

Throughout its history Bologna has always been a city split between nomads and sedentary people. The first university of the world (which is said to have been founded here) was created by a crowd of nomads and monks who came from all over Europe in order to listen to savants and poets and doctors. Roaming clerics came from German towns, Arabian deserts, Andalusia, Sicily, and Polish lands.

During the modern age Bologna has been able to thrive thanks to a precarious balance of nomad workers and merchants and sedentary farmers and bankers. Nomads are nowadays the students, the searchers, the migrant workers who live in the city for a short or a long period, but never really become insiders. The nomads bring knowledge, money and energy. The sedentary population hold the power and exploit the nomads (students pay an incredibly high rent for a bedroom). It's not fair, but it works in general.

Sometimes the relationships go bad, and things deteriorate in the city. In spring 1977 in Bologna there was a certain kind of excitation because of all those ideas circulating in the neuro-sphere.

The university was filled with *terroni* (people originating from the South), Germans, comedians, musicians and cartoonists like Andrea Pazienza and Filippo Scozzari. Artists were squatting houses in the center of the city, and running creative places such as Radio Alice and Traumfabrik.

Some people were reading books like *Anti-Oedipus*, some were reciting poems by Majakovski and Artaud, listening to the music of Keith Jarrett and The Ramones, and inhaling dream inducing substances. The social situation was tight. All over the world the economic recession was raging. *Terroni* students were living four to a room. The PCI was allied with the Christian Democrats, and the political regime in Italy was becoming a conservative block, right wing and left wing united against the social uprising. The Bolognese Communist Party launched campaigns against the provocateurs, and accused the students of being paid by foreign countries' secret services.

Yet in that year that party started to decline in Bologna as in Poland and Czechoslovakia, wherever the Stalinist parties had oppressed people with violence and conformism.

From ironic messages to hyperbolic messages

In February to March 1977 a tiny group of semio-saboteurs were able to transform social conflicts into unpredictable events through the disruption of urban daily life and the détournement of media messages. At the end of February *A/traverso* launched a new magazine, with a long hyperbolic title, 'The revolution is just, possible and necessary: look comrades, the revolution is probable.' It issued a number of demands such as:

We want to expropriate all the assets of the Catholic Church
Cut the working hours, increase the number of jobs
Increase the amount of the salary
Transform production and place it under workers' control
Liberation of the huge amount of intelligence that is wasted by capitalism: Technology has been used so far as a means of control and exploitation. It wants to be turned into a tool for liberation. Working less is possible thanks to the application of cybernetics and informatics.
Zerowork for income
Automate all production
All power to living labor
All work to dead labor

Writing these high sounding proclamations we knew that we were playing with words as if we played with fire. And fire broke out.

On March 11th a student was killed by the police in Bologna during a demonstration. The following afternoon everywhere in the university meetings of students and workers decided to fight back: tens of thousands of people flooded the streets of the city, destroying the shop windows of the rich boutiques and of the banks.

On March 12th the flood invaded the streets of many cities. While in Bologna the students barricaded the street around the occupied university, in Rome a hundred thousand people gathered for demonstration and for a fight. And then the powers of repression struck back.

Radio Alice was shut by the police in the night of March 12th. During the following days the radio was reopened and shut again several times. Those people found in the radio station were arrested and were remanded in jail during the following months. Bookstores were searched.

Hundreds of militants were jailed.

In July a group of French intellectuals including Guattari, Deleuze, Barthes, Sartre, Sollers, Kristeva launched a manifesto against the repression in Italy. The movement decided to call for an international meeting on the same subject. The repression was becoming the major concern, and this was the beginning of the defeat.

The summer issue of *A/traverso* carried a title which was perceived as a provocation: 'The revolution is over. We won.'

This title was not only a provocation. It was also an assessment of the meaning of autonomous action: the rebellion is not a means towards political power. Revolution is not about the collapse of the state. The best way to define the new rebellion is the Deleuzian concept of line of flight: exodus from the kingdom of exploitation and the creation of a new social sphere, which has nothing to do with power, labor or the market. Indeed the following issue of *A/traverso* carried the title: 'Please do not take power.'

Don't worry about your future, you don't have one

The French intellectuals' declaration provoked a debate on the question of the intellectuals and their place in modern society. Following the publication of the declaration we launched a meeting against the repression. And the meeting took place in Bologna in September 1977. One hundred thousand people gathered there for three days to discuss everything: the past and the present of the revolutionary project, repression and desire, armed struggle and nonviolence, and old and new forms of organization.

People coming to Bologna were expecting to find there the magic word opening the way to the next phase of the movement. But nobody spoke this magic word, nobody had the solution: the capitalist counterattack was in the making, and the repression was pushing more and more young people in the ranks of the Red Brigades and the other armed organizations. The cultural counterrevolution was being prepared. In the following years it opened the way to the individual repenting, to heroin, to loneliness, and terror.

Launching a meeting on the subject of repression was not a good idea. So many people were jailed that we thought it was the main concern. But it wasn't. The main subject ought not to have been repression, but the way of escaping the coming capitalist restoration, the possibility of launching a new idea of autonomy. Focusing on the subject of repression opened the way to the military counter-position, and to the growing violence and despair. But the memory of that year has not been cancelled, because hope in a world where friendship prevails over competition and joy prevails over oppression cannot be cancelled. This is why 1977 will always be around the corner, it's the coming revolution.

The nightmare after the end of the dream

In September Hans Martin Schleyer, a former officer of the SS and an NSDAP member who was then president of the German Employers' Association (and thus one of the most powerful industrialists in West Germany) was abducted in a violent kidnapping by militants of the Rote Armee Fraktion.

A letter then arrived at the Federal Government demanding the release of eleven detainees, including the leaders of the RAF who were held in the prison of Stammheim.

The crisis dragged on for more than a month, while the Bundeskriminalamt carried out its biggest investigation to date. Matters escalated when, on October 13th, 1977, Lufthansa Flight 181 from Palma de Mallorca to Frankfurt was hijacked. A group of four Arabs took control of the plane named Landshut. The leader introduced himself to the passengers as 'Captain Mahmud' who would be later identified as Zohair Youssef Akache. When the plane landed in Rome for refueling, he issued the same demands as the Schleyer kidnappers plus the release of two Palestinians held in Turkey, and payment of fifteen million US dollars.

A high-risk rescue operation was led by Hans-Jürgen Wischnewski, then undersecretary in the chancellor's office, who had secretly been flown in from Bonn. At five minutes past midnight on October 18th, the plane was stormed in a seven minute assault by the GSG 9, an elite unit of the German federal police. All four hijackers were shot; three of them died on the spot. Not one passenger was seriously hurt and Wischnewski was able to phone Schmidt and tell the Bonn crisis squad that the operation had been a success.

Half an hour later, German radio broadcasted the news of the rescue, to which the Stammheim inmates listened on their radios. In the course of the night, Baader was found dead with a gunshot wound in the back of his head and Ensslin hanged in her cell; Raspe died in hospital the next day from a gunshot to the head. Irmgard Möller, who had several stab wounds in the chest, survived and was released from prison in 1994.

On October 18th, Hanns-Martin Schleyer was shot dead by his captors on route to Mulhouse, France. The next day, Schleyer's kidnappers announced that he had been "executed" and pinpointed his location. His body was recovered later that day in the trunk of a green Audi 100 on the rue Charles Péguy.

Charlie Chaplin, the man who had recounted the dehumanization of the industrial process, and who had shown the kindness of people who were able to be human although they were poor, died on December 25th. There was no more place for kindness in the world. In the final days of 1977 the movie *Saturday Night Fever* showed a new working class, happy to be exploited all week long in exchange for some fun in the disco.

1977 was the year of mass youth suicide in Japan: the official figure being 784. What caused an outcry was the fast succession, at the end of the summer holidays of that year, of suicides by children: thirteen, to be exact, all amongst primary school children. What is disconcerting here is not so much the number as the gratuitousness and the incomprehensibility of the gesture: in all these cases, there are no motivations or reasons for the act. There is a striking lack of words, an incapacity on the part of the adults that lived with their child to predict, understand, or explain what happened.

In Japan as in Europe and the USA, 1977 is the year of passage beyond modernity. But whereas in Europe, this passage is signaled by the philosophy of authors such as Baudrillard, Virilio, Guattari, Deleuze, and by the political consciousness of mass movements such as the creative Italian *autonomia* or London punk, and whereas in North America it takes the form of a cultural explosion, of a movement of urban transformations which is expressed in the artistic and musical 'no wave,' in Japan, the passage already appears without mediation, as an unexplainable monstrosity which quickly becomes daily normality, the prevalent form of collective existence.

Since 1977, the collapse of the Western mind has assumed a sneaking, subterranean, episodic trajectory, but at the threshold of the millennium, it takes on the rhythm of a precipice, of a no longer containable catastrophe. What the consciousness of 1977 had signaled as a danger and a possibility implicit in the acceleration of productive and existential rhythms, becomes daily news. Certain events signaled this passage, becoming viruses, carrying information that reproduces, proliferates and infects the entire social organism. The exceptional event of the Twin Towers crashing in a cloud of dust following the deadly suicide of nineteen young Muslims is certainly the most impressive, the image-event that spectacularly inaugurates the new times. But the Columbine school massacre, which took place some years before, might have carried a more uncanny message, because it spoke of daily life, of American normality, of the normality of a humanity that has lost all relation with what used to be human and that stumbles along looking for some impossible reassurance in search of a substitute for emotions which it no longer knows.

The year of premonition

We can see 1977 as the year of the last movement of proletarians against the capitalist rule, but also as the year of the announcement of the end of the modern age, the sudden consciousness that in the sphere of modernity no more future is given. The culture of that year is not only involves a critique of the capitalist society, but also a critique of modernity. Here also lies the root of the ambiguity of that culture, the double edge of a certain romantic communitarianism which has opened the way to the right wing reclamation of traditional values.

In the culture of that generation of rebels who read Heidegger and Nietzsche, Burroughs and Philip K Dick, there was a new consciousness that capitalism is organic to the anthropological forms that modernity is made of. The problem of technics is put on the table by the movement of the refusal of work. Technology is not viewed as a mere system of tools, but is perceived as a totalizing dimension, opening infinite possible bifurcations, and simultaneously imposing an inescapable framework of economic constraints. The end of futures that the culture of that year intuited was this closure of the horizon of possibilities. This is why the parable of 1977 is going from utopian rebellion to the clear-eyed despair of impending dystopian developments.

The movement of 1977 proclaimed that 'Democracy is dying,' and it was accused of being anti-democratic. We were only remarking on a trend: the politics of representation is working falsely. Democracy is becoming more an empty ritual, devoid of the ability to deliver true alternatives and true choices.

In the sphere of modernity, politics was decision and choice between alternatives, but since capitalism is able to conjugate the power of economy and the potency of techne, the efficacy of political decision is bound to vanish.

Today, thirty years later, the depletion of politics is revealed and evident. The marriage of economy and techne has made democracy a dead word. 1977 was the sudden consciousness that history is becoming a chain of irreversible automatisms. What capitalism has written in the body and in the brain of the human beings has become part of the genetic store.

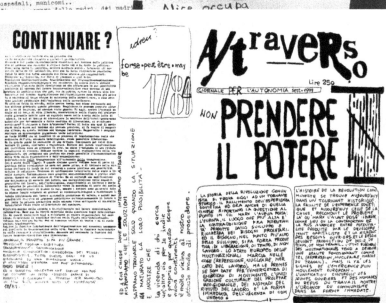

2. Info-labor and 'precarization'

We have no future because our present is too volatile. We have only risk-management. The spinning of the given moment's scenarios. – William Gibson, *Pattern recognition*

In February 2003 the American journalist Bob Herbert published in the *New York Times* the results of a cognitive survey on a sample of hundreds of unemployed youths in Chicago: none of their interviewees expected to find work the next few years, none of them expected to be able to rebel, or to set off large scale collective change. The general sense of the interviews was a sentiment of profound impotence. The perception of decline did not seem focused on politics, but on a deeper cause, the scenario of a social and psychical involution that seems to cancel every possibility of building alternatives.

The fragmentation of the present time is reversed in the implosion of the future.

In *The Corrosion of Character: The Personal Consequences of Work in the New Capitalism*(1988), Richard Sennett reacts to this existential condition of precariousness and fragmentation with nostalgia for a past epoch in which life was structured in relatively stable social roles, and time had enough linear consistency to construe paths of identity.

The arrow of time is broken: in an economy under constant restructuring that is based on the short-term and hates routine, definite trajectories no longer exist. People miss stable human relations and long-term objectives (1988).

But this nostalgia has no hold on present reality, and the attempts to reactivate the community remain artificial and sterile.

In her essay "Precari-us?" (2005) Angela Mitropoulos observes that precariousness is a precarious notion. This because it defines its object in an approximate manner, but also because from this notion derive paradoxical, self-contradictory, in other words precarious strategies. If we concentrate our critical attention on the precarious character of job performance what would our proposed objective be? That of a stable job, guaranteed for life? Naturally no, this would be a cultural regression that would definitely subordinate the role of work. Some started to speak of 'flexicurity' to mean forms of wage independent of job performance. But we are still far from having a strategy of social recomposition for the labor movement to extricate ourselves from unlimited exploitation. We need to resume the thread of analysis of social composition and decomposition if we want to distinguish possible lines of a process of recomposition to come.

In the 1970s, the energy crisis, the consequent economic recession and finally the substitution of work with numerical machines resulted in the formation of a large number of people with no guarantees. Since then the question of precariousness has become central to social analysis, but also in the ambitions of the movement. We began by proposing to struggle for forms of guaranteed income uncoupled from work, in order to face the fact that a large part of the young population had no prospect of guaranteed employment. The situation has changed since then, because what seemed a marginal and temporary condition has now become the prevalent form of labor relations. Precariousness is no longer a marginal and provisional characteristic, but it is the general form of the labor relation in a productive, digitalized sphere, reticular and recombinative.

The word 'precariat' generally stands for the area of work that is no longer definable by fixed rules relative to the labor relation, to salary and to the length of the working day. However if we analyze the past we see that these rules functioned only for a limited period in the history of relations between labor and capital. Only for a short period at the heart of the twentieth century, under the political pressures of unions and workers, in conditions of (almost) full employment and thanks to a more or less strongly regulatory role of the state in the economy, some limits to the natural violence of capitalist dynamics could be legally established. The legal obligations that in certain periods have protected society from the violence of capital were always founded on the existence of a relation of a force of a political and material kind (workers' violence against the violence of capital). Thanks to political force it became possible to affirm rights, establish laws and protect them as personal rights. With the decline in the political force of the workers' movement, the natural precariousness of labor relations in capitalism, and its brutality, have reemerged.

The new phenomenon is not the precarious character of the job market, but the technical and cultural conditions in which info-labor is made precarious. The technical conditions are those of digital recombination of info-work in networks. The cultural conditions are those of the education of the masses and the expectations of consumption inherited from late twentieth century society and continuously fed by the entire apparatus of marketing and media communication.

If we analyze the first aspect, i.e. the technical transformations introduced by the digitalization of the productive cycle, we see that the essential point is not the becoming precarious of the labor relation (which, after all, has always been precarious), but the dissolution of the person as active productive agent, as labor power. We have to look at the cyberspace of global production as an immense expanse of depersonalized human time.

Info-labor, the provision of time for the elaboration and the recombination of segments of info-commodities, is the extreme point of arrival of the process of the abstraction from concrete activities that Marx analyzed as a tendency inscribed in the capital-labor relation.

The process of abstraction of labor has progressively stripped labor time of every concrete and individual particularity. The atom of time of which Marx speaks is the minimal unit of productive labor. But in industrial production, abstract labor time was impersonated by a physical and juridical bearer, embodied in a worker in flesh and bone, with a certified and political identity. Naturally capital did not purchase a personal disposition, but the time for which the workers were its bearers. But if capital wanted to dispose of the necessary time for its valorization, it was indispensable to hire a human being, to buy all of its time, and therefore needed to face up to the material needs and trade union and political demands of which the human was a bearer.

When we move into the sphere of info-labor there is no longer a need to have bought a person for eight hours a day indefinitely. Capital no longer recruits people, but buys packets of time, separated from their interchangeable and occasional bearers.

Depersonalized time has become the real agent of the process of valorization, and depersonalized time has no rights, nor any demands. It can only be either available or unavailable, but the alternative is purely theoretical because the physical body despite not being a legally recognized person still has to buy food and pay rent.

The informatic procedures of the recombination of semiotic material have the effect of liquefying the objective time necessary to produce the info-commodity. The human machine is there, pulsating and available, like a brain-sprawl in waiting. The extension of time is meticulously cellularized: cells of productive time can be mobilized in punctual, casual and fragmentary forms. The recombination of these fragments is automatically realized in the network. The mobile phone is the tool that makes possible the connection between the needs of semio-capital and the mobilization of the living labor of cyberspace. The ringtone of the mobile phone calls the workers to reconnect their abstract time to the reticular flux.

It's a strange word, that with which we identify the ideology prevalent in the post-human transition to digital slavery: liberalism. Liberty is its foundational myth, but the liberty of whom? The liberty of capital, certainly. Capital must be absolutely free to expand in every corner of the world to find the fragment of human time available to be exploited for the most miserable wage. But liberalism also predicates the liberty of the person. The juridical person is free to express itself, to choose its representatives, to be entrepreneurial at the level of politics and the economy.

Very interesting. Only the person has disappeared. What is left is like an inert object, irrelevant and useless. The person is free, sure. But his time is enslaved. His liberty is a juridical fiction to which nothing in concrete daily life corresponds. If we consider the conditions in which the work of the majority of humanity, proletariat and cognitariat, is actually carried out in our time, if we examine the conditions the average wage globally, if we consider the current and now largely realized cancellation of previous labor rights, we can say with no rhetorical exaggeration that we live in a regime of slavery. The average salary on the global level is hardly sufficient to buy the indispensable means for the mere survival of a person whose time is at the service of capital. And people do not have any right over the time of which they are formally the proprietors, but effectively expropriated. That time does not really belong to them, because it is separated from the social existence of the people who make it available to the recombinative cyber-productive circuit. The time of work is fractalized, that is, reduced to minimal fragments that can be reassembled, and the fractalization makes it possible for capital to constantly find the conditions of minimum salary.

How can we oppose the decimation of the working class and its systemic depersonalization, the slavery that is affirmed as a mode of command of precarious and depersonalized work? This is the question that is posed with insistence by whoever still has a sense of human dignity. Nevertheless the answer does not come out because the form of resistance and of struggle that were efficacious in the twentieth century no longer appear to have the capacity to spread and consolidate themselves, nor consequently can they stop the absolutism of capital. An experience that derives from workers' struggle in recent years is that the struggle of precarious workers does not make a cycle. Fractalized work can also punctually rebel, but this does not set into motion any wave of struggle. The reason is easy to understand. In order for struggles to form a cycle there must be a spatial proximity of the bodies of labor and an existential temporal continuity. Without this proximity and this continuity, we lack the conditions for the cellularized bodies to become community. No wave can be created, because the workers do not share their existence in time, and behaviors can only become a wave when there is a continuous proximity in time that info-labor no longer allows.

Skizo-economy

The categories of the critique of political economy are now insufficient because processes of subjectivation traverse fields that are much more complex. A new disciplinary field is starting to be delineated in the encounter between the territories of economics, semiotics and psycho-chemistry.

Semio-capital is capital-flux that coagulates in semiotic artifacts without materializing itself. The concepts forged by two centuries of economic thought seem dissolved, inoperative and incapable of comprehending a great deal of the phenomena that have emerged in the sphere of social production since it became cognitive. Cognitive activity has always been the basis of all human production, even that of a more mechanical type. There is no process of human labor that does not imply an exercise of intelligence. But today, cognitive capacity is becoming the essential productive resource. In the sphere of industrial labor, the mind was put to work as a repetitive automatism, the physiological support of muscular movement. Today the mind is at work in so many innovations, languages and communicative relations. The subsumption of the mind in the process of capitalist valorization leads to a true mutation. The conscious and sensitive organism is submitted to a competitive pressure, to an acceleration of stimuli, to a constant attentive stress. As a consequence, the mental atmosphere, the info-sphere in which the mind is formed and enters into relations with other minds, becomes a psychopathogenic atmosphere. To understand semio-capital's infinite game of mirrors we must outline a new disciplinary field, delimited by three aspects:

–the critique of the political economy of connective intelligence;
–the semiology of linguistic-economic fluxes;
–the psychochemistry of the info-spheric atmosphere that studies the psychopathogenic effects of economic development on the human mind.

The process of digital production is taking a biological form which can be likened to an organism: the nervous system of an organization is analogous with the human nervous system. Every industrial enterprise has 'autonomic' systems, operational processes that must function for its survival. What was lacking from organizations in the past were the links between pieces of information that resemble the interconnected neurons in the brain. The networked digital business functions as an excellent artificial nervous system. Information flows within it quickly and naturally, like thought in a human being, and we are able to use technology to govern and co-ordinate groups of people, with the same rapidity with which we can concentrate on a problem. According to Bill Gates (1999), the conditions are created for the realization of a new form of economic system, centered on what can be defined as "Business at the speed of thought."

In the connected world, the retroactive loops of general systems theory are fused with the dynamic logic of biogenetics in a post-human vision of digital production. Human minds and flesh are integrated with digital circuits thanks to interfaces of acceleration and simplification: a model of bio-info production is emerging that produces semiotic artifacts with the capacity for the auto-replication of living systems. Once fully operative, the digital nervous system can be rapidly installed in every form of organization. This means that *only apparently* Microsoft concerns itself with software, products and services. In reality, the hidden finality of software production is the wiring of the human mind in a network continuum of the cybernetic type destined to structure the fluxes of digital information by means of the nervous system of all the key institutions of contemporary life. Microsoft will therefore be considered as a global virtual memory, exchangeable and ready to install. A cyber-panopticon inserted in the fleshy circuits of human subjectivity. Cybernetics finally becomes life, or, as Bill Gates likes to say, "information is our vital fluid."

The psychic collapse of the economy

The digital nervous system incorporates itself progressively in the organic nervous system, in the circuit of human communication, and recodifies it according to its operational lines and according to its own speed. But in order to fulfill this transformation, the body-mind must pass through an infernal mutation, that we see developing in the history of the world. To understand and to analyze this process, neither the conceptual instruments of political economy nor the instruments of technological analysis are sufficient. The process of production becomes semiotic and the formation of the digital nervous system co-involves and enervates the mind, the social psyche, desires and hopes, fears and imaginings. Therefore if we want to analyze these productive transformations, we must concern ourselves with semiotic production, with linguistic and cognitive mutations. And mutation passes through the range of pathologies.

Neoliberal culture has injected into the social brain a constant stimulus towards competition and the technical system of the digital network has rendered possible an intensification of informatic stimuli, transmitted from the social brain to individual brains. This acceleration of stimuli is a pathogenic factor that has wide ranging effects in society. Economic competition and digital intensification of informatic stimuli, combined together, induce a state of permanent electrocution that flows into a widespread pathology which manifests itself either in the panic syndrome or in attention disorders.

Panic is an ever more widespread syndrome. Until a few years ago, psychiatrists hardly recognized this symptom that belonged rather to the romantic literary imagination, and could approach the feeling of being overwhelmed by the infinite richness of the forms of nature by unlimited cosmic power. Today, instead, panic is ever more frequently denounced as a painful and worrying symptom, the physical sensation of no longer succeeding in governing one's own body, an acceleration of the heart rate, a shortness of breath that can lead to fainting and paralysis. Even if to my knowledge exhaustive research does not exist in this area, the hypothesis can be proposed that the mediatization of communication and the consequent rarefaction of physical contact, can provoke pathologies in the affective and emotional sphere. For the first time in human history, there is a generation that has learnt more words and heard more stories from the televisual machine than from its mother. Attention disturbances are more and more widespread. Millions of North American and European children are treated for a disturbance that manifests itself as the incapacity to maintain concentrated attention on an object for more than a few seconds. The constant excitation of the mind on the part of neurostimulant fluxes probably leads to a pathological saturation. If we want to understand the contemporary economy we must concern ourselves with the psychopathology of relations. And if we want to understand contemporary psychochemistry we must take into account the fact that the mind is invested by semiotic fluxes that follow an extra-semiotic principle: the principle of economic competition, the principle of maximum development. From the time when capitalism connected to the brain, the latter incorporated a pathological agent, a psychotic meme that will accelerate pulsations even to tremors, even to collapse.

In the 1990s, Prozac culture was intermingled with the new economy. Hundreds of thousands of operators, directors and managers of the occidental economy took innumerable decisions in a state of chemical euphoria and psychopharmacological lightheadedness. But in the long term the organism collapsed, unable to support indefinitely the chemical euphoria that had sustained competitive enthusiasm and productivist fanaticism. Collective attention was supersaturated and this was provoking a collapse of a social and economic kind. As happens in a manic depressive organism, as happens with a patient affected by *bipolar disorder*, after the financial euphoria of the 1990s, there followed a depression. It is therefore a case of clinical depression that strikes motivation, initiative, self-esteem, desire and sex appeal at the roots. To understand the crisis of the new economy it is necessary to begin from the psychic experience of the virtual class, it is necessary to reflect on the psychic and emotional state of the millions of cognitive workers who animated the scene of business, culture and the imaginary during the decade of the 1990s. The individual psychic depression of a single cognitive worker is not a consequence of the economic crisis but its cause. It would be simple to consider depression as a consequence of a bad business cycle. After having worked for so many years happily and profitably, the value of shares has plummeted and our brainworker is overcome by an ugly depression. It does not happen in this way. Depression descends on the cognitive worker because his or her own emotional, physical, intellectual system cannot indefinitely support the hyperactivity provoked by the market and by pharmaceuticals. As a consequence, things are set to go badly in the market. What is the market? The market is the place in which signs and nascent meanings, desires and projections meet. If we want to speak of demand and supply, we must reason in terms of fluxes of desire and semiotic attractors that formerly had appeal and today have lost it.

In the net economy, flexibility has evolved into a form of fractalization of work. Fractalization means the modular and recombinant fragmentation of the time of activity. The worker no longer exists as a person. He or she is only an interchangeable producer of microfragments of recombinant semiosis that enter into the continuous flux of the Net. Capital no longer pays for the availability of a worker to be exploited for a long period of time; it no longer pays a salary that covers the entire range of economic needs of a person who works. The worker (a machine endowed with a brain that can be used for fragments of time) becomes paid for his or her occasional, temporary services. Work time is fragmented and cellularized. Cells of time are for sale on the Net and businesses can buy as much as they want without being obligated in any way in the social protection of the worker.

The intense and prolonged investment of mental and libidinal energies in the labor process has created the conditions for a psychic collapse that is transferred into the economic field with the recession and the fall in demand and into the political field in the form of military aggressivity. The use of the word collapse is not as a metaphor but as a clinical description of what is happening in the occidental mind. The word collapse expresses a real and exact pathological phenomenon that invests the psycho-social organism. That which we have seen in the period following the first signs of economic decline, in the first months of the new century, is a psychopathic phenomenon of over-excitation, trembling, panic and finally of a depressive fall. The phenomena of economic depression have always contained elements of the crisis of the psychosocial equilibrium, but when at last the process of production has involved the brain in a massive way, psychopathology has become the crucial aspect of economic cycles.

The available attention time for the workers involved in the informatic cycle is constantly being reduced: they are involved in a growing number of mental tasks that occupy every fragment of their attention time. For them there is no longer the time to dedicate to love, to tenderness, to affection. They take Viagra because they don't have time for sexual preliminaries. They take cocaine to be continuously alert and reactive. They take Prozac to cancel out the awareness of the senselessness that unexpectedly empties their life of any interest. Cellularization has brought about a type of permanent occupation of living time. The effect is a mutation of social relations in a psychopathic direction. The signs are evident: millions of packets of psycho-pharmaceuticals sold, an epidemic of attention disturbances spreading among children and adolescents, the becoming normal of the diffusion of drugs like Ritalin in schools and what seems to be the spreading of an epidemic of panic in the fabric of everyday life.

The info-sphere and the social mind

The mediascape is the universe of transmitters that send to our brain signals according to the most varied formats. The info-sphere is the interface between the media system and the mind that receives the signals, the mental ecosphere, that immaterial sphere in which semiotic fluxes interact with the reception antennae of the minds scattered on the planet. The mind is the universe of receivers that are not naturally limited to receiving but process, create and in their turn put in motion new processes of transmission and provoke the continuous evolution of the mediascape.

The evolution of the info-sphere's activation of always more complex networks of information distribution has produced a leap in the power, speed and the very format of the info-sphere. There is no corresponding leap in the power and format of reception.

The universe of receivers, human brains of real people made of flesh, fragile and sensual organs, is not formatted according to the same standard as the system of digital transmitters. The functional paradigm of the universe of transmitters does not correspond to the functional paradigm of the universe of receivers. This asymmetry is manifested by various pathological effects: permanent electrocution, panic, over-excitation, hyper-mobility, attention disturbances, dyslexia, information overload and saturation of reception circuits.

At the origin of this saturation, there is a real and proper deformity of formats. The format of the universe of transmitters has evolved, multiplying its powers, while the format of the universe of receivers has not been able to evolve in as rapid a manner, for the simple reason that it is based on an organic support (the human brain-body) that has evolutionary times completely different from the evolutionary times of machines.

That which is being determined could be defined as a paradigmatic discrepancy, a schism between the paradigm that models the universe of transmitters and the paradigm that models the universe of receivers. In a situation like this, communication becomes an asymmetrical disturbed process. We could speak in this regard of a discrepancy between cyberspace in unlimited and constant expansion and cybertime. Cyberspace is a network that includes mechanical and organic components whose processing power can be accelerated without limits, while cybertime is an essentially lived reality, linked to an organic support (the human body and brain) whose processing time cannot be accelerated beyond relatively rigid natural limits.

Since the time when, in 1977, he wrote the book *Speed and Politics*, Paul Virilio has maintained that speed is the decisive factor in modern history. It is thanks to speed, Virilio claims, that wars are won, both military and commercial ones. In many of his writings, Virilio shows that the speed of movements, of transportation, of motorization has allowed armies to win wars in the course of the last century. Since then, it has been possible to substitute objects, goods and people for signs. By virtual, electronically transferable phantasms, the barriers of speed have been broken and the most impressive process of acceleration that human history has ever known has erupted. In a certain sense we can say that space no longer exists, given that information can cross it instantly and events can be transferred in real time from one place to another on the planet, becoming virtually shared events. But what are the consequences of this acceleration on the human mind, on the human body? To understand it we must make reference to the capacity of conscious processing, to the capacity for affective assimilation of signs and events on the part of the conscious and sensitive organism.

The acceleration of information exchange has produced and is producing an effect of a pathological type on the individual human mind and even more on the collective mind. Individuals are not in a position to consciously process the immense and always growing mass of information that enters their computers, their cell phones, their television screens, their electronic diaries and their heads. However, it seems indispensable to follow, recognize, evaluate, process all this information if you want to be efficient, competitive, victorious. The practice of *multitasking*, the opening of a window of hypertextual attention, the passage from one context to another for the complex evaluation of processes, tends to deform the sequential modality of mental processing. According to Christian Marazzi, who has concerned himself in various books with the relations between economics, language and affectivity, the latest generation of economic operators is affected by a real and proper form of dyslexia, incapable of reading a page from the beginning to the end according to sequential procedures, incapable of maintaining concentrated attention on the same object for a long time. And dyslexia spreads to cognitive and social behaviors, leading to rendering the pursuit of linear strategies nearly impossible.

Some, like Davenport and Beck , speak of an attention economy. But when a cognitive faculty enters into and becomes part of economic discourse this means that it has become a scarce resource. The necessary time for paying attention to the fluxes of information to which we are exposed and which must be evaluated in order to be able to make decisions is lacking. The consequence is in front of our eyes: political and economic decisions no longer respond to a long term strategic rationality and simply follow immediate interests. On the other hand, we are always less available for giving our attention to others gratuitously. We no longer have the attention time for love, tenderness, nature, pleasure and compassion. Our attention is ever more besieged and therefore we assign it only to our careers, to competition and to economic decisions. And in any case our temporality cannot follow the insane speed of the hyper-complex digital machine. Human beings tend to become the ruthless executors of decisions taken without attention.

The universe of transmitters, or cyberspace, now proceeds at a superhuman velocity and becomes untranslatable for the universe of receivers, or cybertime, that cannot go faster than what is allowed by the physical material from which our brain is made, the slowness of our body, the need for caresses and affection. Thus opens a pathological gap and mental illness spreads as testified by the statistics and above all our everyday experience. And just as pathology spreads, so too do drugs. The flourishing industry of psychopharmaceuticals beats records every year, the number of packets of Ritalin, Prozac, Zoloft and other psychotropics sold in the pharmacies continually increases, while dissociation, suffering, desperation, terror, the desire not to exist, to not have to fight continuously, to disappear grows alongside the will to kill and to kill oneself.

When, towards the end of the 1970s, an acceleration of the productive and communicative rhythms in occidental metropolitan centers was imposed, a gigantic epidemic of drug addiction made its appearance. The world was leaving its human epoch to enter the era of machinic post-human acceleration: many sensitive organisms of the human variety began to snort cocaine, a substance that permits the acceleration of the existential rhythm leading to transforming oneself into a machine. Many other sensitive organisms of the human kind injected heroin in their veins, a substance that deactivates the relation with the speed of the surrounding atmosphere. The epidemic of powders during the 1970s and the 1980s produced an existential and cultural devastation with which we still haven't come to terms with. Then illegal drugs were replaced by those legal substances which the pharmaceutical industry in a white coat made available for its victims and this was the epoch of anti-depressants, of euphorics and of mood regulators.

Today psychopathy reveals itself ever more clearly as a social epidemic and, more precisely, a socio-communicational one. If you want to survive you have to be competitive and if you want to be competitive you must be connected, receive and process continuously an immense and growing mass of data. This provokes a constant attentive stress, a reduction of the time available for affectivity. These two tendencies, inseparably linked, provoke an effect of devastation on the individual psyche: depression, panic, anxiety, the sense of solitude and existential misery. But these individual symptoms cannot be indefinitely isolated, as psychopathology has done up until now and as economic power wishes to do. It is not possible to say: "You are exhausted, go and take a vacation at Club Med, take a pill, make a cure, get the hell away from it all, recover in the psychiatric hospital, kill yourself." It is no longer possible, for the simple reason that it is no longer a matter of a small minority of crazies or a marginal amount of depressives. It concerns a growing mass of existential misery that is tending always more to explode in the center of the social system. Besides, it is necessary to consider a decisive fact: at the time when capital needed to suck in physical energy from its exploited and from its slaves, psychopathology could be relatively marginalized. Your psychic suffering didn't matter much to capital when you only had to insert screws and handle a lathe. You could be as sad as a solitary fly in a bottle, but your productivity was hardly affected because your muscles could still function. Today capital needs mental energies, psychic energies. And these are exactly the capacities that are fucking up. It's because of this that psychopathology is exploding in the center of the social scene. The economic crisis depends for the most part on a circulation of sadness, depression, panic and demotivation. The crisis of the new economy was provoked in a large part by a crisis of motivations, by a fall the artificial euphoria of the 1990s. This has led to effects of disinvestment and in part even to a reduction of consumption. In general, unhappiness functions as a stimulus to consume: buying is a suspension of anxiety, an antidote to loneliness, but only up to a certain point. Beyond this certain point, suffering becomes a demotivating factor for purchasing. There is therefore an elaboration of conflicting strategies.

The masters of the world certainly do not want humanity to be able to be happy, because a happy humanity would not let itself be caught up in productivity, in the discipline over work or in hypermarkets. However, they try out useful techniques to make unhappiness moderate and tolerable, for postponing or preventing a suicidal explosion, for inducing consumption.

What strategies will the collective organism follow in order to escape this fabric of unhappiness? Is a strategy of deceleration, of the reduction of complexity possible and able to be hypothesized? I don't believe so. In human society, potentialities cannot be definitively canceled out, even when they are revealed to be lethal for the individual and probably even for the species. These potentials become regulated and kept under control for as long as possible, but in the end are inevitably used as happened (and will happen again) with the atomic bomb. A strategy of the *upgrading* of the human organism is possible – of the mechanical adjustment of the human body and brain to a hyperfast info-sphere. This is the strategy that is used to define the *post-human*. Finally a strategy of subtraction is possible, of distancing from the vortex, but this is a type of strategy that only small communities can follow, constituting spheres of existential, economic, and informatic autonomy with respect to the economic world.

Panic war and semio-capital

Globalization stands reframed in the dark light of the global war. This means we need to reconceptualize the change that is taking place in the social, economic and anthropological form of globalization. During the past two centuries, global control was the general techno-utopia of capitalist society and modern culture. Now, the time of global control is over. We are completely out of this framework today. The new governing framework of capitalism is global panic. If we want to understand what panic means we have to talk about the attention economy and about 'digital labor.' This is where the source of contemporary panic lies: in the organization of time in the digital sphere, in the relationship between cyberspace and cybertime.

What is panic? We are told that psychiatrists have recently discovered and named a new kind of disorder – they call it Panic Syndrome. It seems that it's something quite recent in the psychological self-perception of human beings. But what does panic mean?

Once, panic used to be a nice word, and this is the sense in which the Swiss-American psychoanalyst James Hillman remembers it in his book on Pan. Pan used to be the god of nature, the god of totality. In Greek mythology, Pan was the symbol of the relationship between man and nature.

Nature is the overwhelming flow of reality, things and information that we are surrounded by. Modern culture is based on the idea of human domination, of the domestication of nature. So the original panic feeling, which was something good for the ancient world, is becoming increasingly terrifying and destructive. Today, panic has become a form of psychopathology. We can speak of panic when we see a conscious organism (individual or social) being overwhelmed by the speed of processes he, she is involved in, and has no time to process the information input. In these cases the organism, all of a sudden, is no more able to process the sheer amount of information coming into its cognitive field or even that which is being generated by the organism itself.

Technological transformations have displaced the focus from the sphere of the production of material goods towards the sphere of semiotic goods: the info-sphere. With this, semio-capital becomes the general form of the economy. The accelerated creation of surplus value depends on the acceleration of the info-sphere. The digitalization of the info-sphere opens the road to this kind of acceleration. Signs are produced and circulated at a growing speed but the human terminal of the system (the embodied mind) is put under growing pressure, and finally it cracks. I think that the current economic crisis has something to do with this imbalance in the field of semio-production and in the field of semio-demand. This imbalance in the relationship between the supply of semiotic goods and the socially available time of attention is the core of the economic crisis as well as the core of the intellectual and the political crises that we are living through now.

We can describe this situation in terms of the relationship between cyberspace and cybertime. Cyberspace is the infinite productivity of collective intelligence in a networked dimension. The potency of the General Intellect is enormously enhanced when a huge number of points enter into connections with each other thanks to the telematic network. Consequently, info-production is able to create an infinite supply of mental and intellectual goods. But while cyberspace is conceptually infinite, cybertime is not infinite at all. I call cybertime the ability of the conscious organism to actually process (cyber-spatial) information. This ability cannot be indefinitely expanded, because it has limits that are physical, emotional, affective. The contradiction between infinite expansion of cyberspace and limited capability of processing of cybertime is the origin of contemporary chaos.

Deleuze and Guattari talk about chaos in *What is Philosophy?*. They say that chaos occurs when the world goes too fast for your brain. This is chaos.

We could recall that Karl Marx had once expressed the concept of an overproduction crisis. You have an overproduction crisis when machinery and the labor of workers produce an amount of goods that the market cannot absorb. During the history of the industrial system, the overproduction crisis was recurrent, and capitalism was pushed to destroy goods, destroy productive capacity, and also destroy human lives, in order to overcome this kind of economic crises.

What is going to happen now? Should we see a relationship between this big imbalance and the war that is raging and obscuring the horizon of the world? Let's go back to the concept of panic.

Semio-capital is in a crisis of overproduction, but the form of this crisis is not only economic, but also psychopathic. Semio-capital, in fact, is not about the production of material goods, but about the production of psychic stimulation. The mental environment is saturated by signs that create a sort of continuous excitation, a permanent electrocution, which leads the individual mind as well as the collective mind to a state of collapse.

The problem of panic is generally connected with the management of time. But we can also see a spatial side to panic. During the past centuries, the building of the modern urban environment used to be dependent on the rationalist plan of the political city. The economic dictatorship of the last few decades has accelerated urban expansion. The interaction between cyber-spatial sprawl and urban physical environment has destroyed the rationalist organization of space.

In the intersection of information and urban space we see the proliferation of a chaotic sprawl following no rule, no plan, dictated by the sole logic of economic interest. Urban panic is caused by the perception of this sprawl and this proliferation of metropolitan experience; the proliferation of spatial lines of flight. The metropolis is a surface of complexity in the territorial domain. The social organism is unable to process the overwhelmingly complex experience of metropolitan chaos. The proliferation of lines of communication has created a new kind of chaotic perception.

In their book *Attention Economy*, Davenport and Bleick say that the central problem of the cognitive worker, and generally of people who are living in hypersaturated informational environments, is this: we have no more time for attention, we are no more able to understand and process information input because our time is saturated by a flow of hyper-information. We don't have time for attention in the workplace. We are forced to process far too large amounts of information and our body-mind is completely taken by this. And further, we have no time for affection, for communication, for erotic relationships. We have no more time for that spatial kind of attention that means attention to the body – to our body, to the body of the other. So, more and more, we feel that we have run out of time; that we must accelerate. And we feel simultaneously that acceleration leads to a loss of life, of pleasure and of understanding.

This collapse in the relationship between cyberspace and cybertime may also be seen as the special feature of the current political situation. The world is rushing into a global war whose reasons are not clear, whose limits are not known. Some are speaking of a long-lasting war, possibly an infinite war. Nonsense? Yes, nonsense. But this nonsensical war is the most alarming symptom of the panic syndrome.

Colin Powell, some days after 9/11, spoke about the rumors that the intelligence services had received some information about bombings and hijackings of airplanes before September 11th. "Yes, it's true", he said, "Yes, it's true, we have received information about something like this, we have received information about bombings and so on. But we always receive lots of information we are not able to process or even to see. We had too much of it, this is the problem. We have too much information."

This is precisely the effect of info-saturation, which is the consequence of the unbounded expansion of cyberspace. On the one hand, war is a way by which capital deals with the economic problems of over-production, investments in weapons and tools for security, security and security. On the other hand, war is made inevitable by the mental confusion of the ruling class. They do not understand what is happening because the reality has become too complex and too aggressive. So they react in a primary way. The world's ruling class is overwhelmed by the very complexity of the world they have built for themselves.

Splatterkapitalismus. The criminal face of contemporary capitalism.

Legend has it that in the early 1960s the young Romano Alquati wandered on a flamboyant scooter along the roads of Piedmont – crisp air, calm horizon and snowy mountain – surrounding Ivrea and Olivetti. 'The labor power and class composition of Olivetti in Ivrea' was written there. In my opinion this essay had the greatest influence on our understanding of late industrial capitalism and the new working class that was about to subvert the existing order of things, society, politics and culture.

On the gloomy horizon of a decaying countryside, amidst the poisonous stench of the dumping grounds, driving a scooter is Roberto Saviano, with the intense and pain ridden glare that I stared at on the back cover of his first book *Gomorra* (2006). *Gomorra* is the first book that tells, with no reassuring ideological fiction, the social and cultural composition of contemporary global capital. Saviano's scooter drives along the artificial hills of the dumping grounds and through the narrow streets of Secondigliano, from whence he saw large crowds of slaves breaking their backs over the countless clandestine laboratories of production of the omnipresent commodity that is suffocating the planet.

The few people who mention this book either say that it is a novel or reportage. In my view it is both, and more: it tries to present a systematic analysis of contemporary capitalism, of its real nature, and of its global, deterritorialized and reticular operations. It is an attempt at systematically analyzing a phenomenon that is all but systematic, an analysis of a system that no longer follows rules, and grounds its efficiency and productivity on this perfect deregulation.

A work like this should be done on many other similar fields. The region of Campania must be seen as the hologram of a planet that capitalist deregulation has handed over to the control of criminal organizations, as in Mexico – where the drugs mafia employs techniques that resemble Al Qaida's – or Columbia, Pakistan, the Gulf of Bengali, the Balkans, or Russia – where the PCUS, without changing its hierarchical structures, has turned into a mafia network that signs contracts worth billions with the obsequious heads of European nations, and where KGB killers eliminate marauders like Yodorkhovski to share the extorted loot with the well-educated managers of ENI and ENEL. Forget Provenzano, forget Riina: Putin and Berlusconi-Prodi don't need to strangle people with their hands; someone can do it for them before the presidents jointly sign the contract.

Saviano describes the paradigmatic functioning of post-bourgeois capitalism and uses this model of analysis to inquire into a particular situation that is linked by thousands of threads to thousands of similar situations. The worst way to read this book is seeing it as the latest Neapolitan sketch, the description of a backward and marginal land, as an example of residual criminality. Italian politicians usually speak of the

South as an excrescence, but this is a lie. An excrescence is something that comes out of a healthy body; here there is no healthy body. The system described by Saviano is the body, as shown by the Tronchetti-Provera's affair, the last of a species of brave captains whom the center-left government gifted with the public company Telecom so that other brave captains could fleece it and then sell it to the best buyer as if it was theirs, whilst it is ours. Our thing, that is, their thing. This is post-bourgeois deregulated capitalism, where murderers are not just an excrescence but the whole body.

Saviano shows us that in Campania the advanced form of the cycle of production of global capitalism manifests itself as a tendency towards which the whole process of production is evolving. The institutional bonzes of the Italian state promise to take action against criminality through the economic development of the South, but criminality is economic development because economic development is no longer anything but criminality.

The enterprise

Efficiency is the decisive trait of all entrepreneurial operations, be it commodity distribution by means of hundreds of lined up HGVs or the melting a couple of cadavers in acid.

> We instructed the purchase of a hundred liters of muriatic acid, we needed two hundred liters metal containers, normally used for keeping petrol and open at the top. In our experience each container needed to be filled with fifty liters of acid and as we planned to suppress two people, we got two barrels ready (2006: 63).

Many questions of efficiency are discussed in this book: only efficiency decides on the economic success of the enterprise.

> The watchword is *laissez fair, laissez-passer*. The theory is that the market regulates itself. So in a short time anyone willing to set up a small trade with friends, anyone who wants to buy for fifteen and sell for a hundred to afford a holiday, a Master's program or mortgage repayments, is attracted to Secondigliano. The absolute liberalization of the commerce of drugs lead to a huge price fall (2006: 78).

Despite its semblance of chaotic wandering through mazes of narrow streets and villages, warehouses and desolate beaches, the book reconstructs some of the commodity cycles on which the system is founded.

> The word 'camorra' doesn't exist; it's a cop's word, used by magistrates and journalists. It makes the affiliates smile, it's an experts' term, relegated to history. The word in use to describe clan members is System: they belong to the system of Secondigliano. It is an eloquent term, referring to a mechanism rather than a structure. Organized criminality directly coincides with the economy, the dialectics of commerce is the bone structure of the clan (2006: 48).

A mechanism rather than a structure, a device, a machinic concatenation capable of generating profits. The components of the device can change without changing its functioning. The abstract character of capitalism, of labor and of the enterprise, is a lesson learned by criminals and now lies at the core of the entrepreneurial system. Purged of any personalistic or family concreteness, it uses people and families to serve a higher purpose: accumulation, growth, and development.

Commodity cycles

In the first part of the book, in the tale of the swarming world of clandestine workers connecting the projectual labor of tailors and the legacy of their local popular tradition with the executive labor of thousands of workers scattered around the world, the author reconstructs the commodity cycle of the textile industry, fashion and creation. The cycle is one of true falsity, or rather of false truth, linked to a trade network analogous to that of any other chain, although it was built on the physical removal of competitors. No one will ever ask you how many people you've strangled if you are the manager of a shopping center that generates profits. And if by an unfortunate chance a magistrate asks you to account for a dozen of cadavers, no problem, the enterprise won't come to a halt because of it. The boss might go to jail, but what matters is that his function continues to function.

Saviano describes the cycle of drugs, the forms of organization of the drugs trade on the ground and the economic dimensions of the die, none of which has anything to do with the marginal dynamics of a ghetto.

> A region capable of generating three hundred million Euros a year from the industry of just one family cannot be a ghetto. A region where tens of clans are operative and profit margins reach those of high finance could not be a ghetto (2006: 81).

When the ministers of trade and industry talk about the GNP they should tell the truth: as the amount of blood shed, the death rates, and the poison increase, so does the GNP grows.

According to official statistics, 20% of the GNP is based on tax evasion: at least a quarter of the wealth produced and exchanged in Italy is generated under conditions of criminality. Murder, the disposal of dead bodies, blackmail and armed gangs should be classified as decisive factors for the GNP formation. They should be regularly included in bookkeeping, if the current state of affairs is to be recognized: if the families of camorra and mafia decided to give up their trades, perhaps as a result of an apparition of Padre Pio, the Italian economy would collapse.

Saviano proceeds in his analysis of the commodity cycle with a brief mention of the arms trade. He reports that Italy spends twenty-seven billion Dollars a year on weapons, more than Russia and twice as much as Israel – the data was gathered by the International Institute of Stockholm as part of their research on peace. Do the people who were put in government by the vote of pacifists know about this?

The cycle of arms is tightly linked to the cycle of extermination that the liberal-camorrist economy is naturally an integral part of. Saviano counts three thousand six hundred casualties over the years, in the camorra region only.

> This is the heart of Europe; here the majority of the national economy is forged. The strategies of its extraction are not important. What matters is that the cannon fodder is kept stuck in the peripheries, kicked in the twines of cement and garbage, in illegal factories and cocaine warehouses. And nobody must point to it, it all has to look like a gang war, a war amongst the ragged and dispossessed (2006: 135).

It is not a gang war, it is normal market competition. It is not the war of the poor; it is the pulsating heart of the national economy.

Entrepreneurs: that is the self-definition of the camorrists of Caserta, nothing but entrepreneurs (2006: 210).

What else should they call themselves? Their enterprise is no different from any other, formal details aside. Regulations are declared to be laces and strings worldwide, for the past thirty years nation states have been preoccupied with just one thing: to lift all the regulations that prevent the free expression of competition or slow down the free flow of labor, the interminable reduction of labor costs.

Compete

The concept of competition has replaced that of competence.

Competence is the intellectual skill that enabled the bourgeoisie to carry out its planning, administrative, and organizational function, and justified its right to property.

Ever since the technologies of intelligence made it possible to standardize the processes of planning, coordination and administration that once coalesced with the role of ownership, intellectual functions have turned into the functions of subordinate labor.

The competent bourgeoisie was replaced by a class that turned competition into the only rule and competence. However, when speaking of competition, is it not obvious that the most competitive is the one who can eliminate the adversaries? And when it comes to eliminating adversaries things get serious.

As property came to coincide with a dusty cloud of fractions of investment rather than with the person, competition replaced competence. Many competences are still necessary to production but they are now detached from the role of the enterprise. Any intellectual competence that is not related to speculation is made precarious, devalued and low waged.

Only those who developed a high skill in the managerial function are able to become wealthy through their labor. What does a managerial function detached from the specificity of concrete intellectual competence consist of? Fabrication, trickery, lies and fraudulent accounting, tax evasion, and, if necessary, the physical removal of competitors, torture, and genocide. In this respect, Halliburton is more efficient and heinous than the Casalei or Corleonesi clans.

Ignorance rises up to power and economic decisions are made purely on the basis of the gain of the maximum and most immediate profit. All that matters is the reduction of labor costs, because this is what competition is about, nothing to do with the production of quality. As a result, the last word on decisions about production does not come from chemists, urbanists or doctors, but from people with managerial competence, that is, with the ability to reduce labor costs and accelerate the realization of profit. The dynamics of neoliberalism have destroyed the bourgeoisie and replaced it with two distinct and opposing classes: the cognitariat on the one hand, i.e. the precarious and cellularized labor of intelligence, and the managerial class on the other, whose only competence is in competitiveness. Taken to its extreme, as evident in increasingly larger regions of global capitalist production, competition becomes the armed removal of competitors, the armed imposition of one supplier, the systematic devastation of everything that does not submit to the profit of the strongest. Who does competition better than those who remove their competitors? And what better techniques for this removal are there than walling up of people alive, slaughtering or dissolving them in muriatic acid? *Gomorra* is inscribed in the genetic code of neoliberalism.

Regulations

The neoliberal phase of capitalism appears to be an interminable and uninterrupted process of *deregulation*, but in fact it is the exact opposite. As all rules of coexistence are abolished, the rules of violence are imposed. As the regulations that set limits to the invasiveness of the principles of competition are removed, hard-and-fast automatisms are introduced in material relations between people, who become more enslaved as the enterprise becomes freer. The process of deregulation unremittingly removes the rules that bridle the mobility of productivity and hinder the expansive power of capital. Forms of social civilization and human rights established throughout modernity are rules that deregulation is set to eliminate. The advance of capitalist deregulation eradicates the cultural and juridical conventions of modernity and bourgeois law one by one. This is why capitalism has turned into a criminal system and keeps working towards the expansion of the realm of pure violence, where its advancement can proceed unhindered. Slatterkapitalismus: the end of bourgeois hegemony and of the enlightened universality of the law.

Crime is no longer a marginal function of the capitalist system, but the decisive winning factor for deregulated competition. Torture, homicide, child exploitation, the drive to prostitution, and the production of instruments of mass destruction have become irreplaceable techniques of economic competition. Crime is best suited to the principle of competition.

Garbage

In conclusion, the last cycle of Splatterkapitalismus, as described by Saviano, is the cycle of waste. Waste is first and foremost the men and women that the process of criminal valorization leaves behind, deformed, burned, thrown in a ditch, made to explode with a hand grenade, or simply humiliated, emptied out, jailed. Unlike the bourgeoisie, who ascribed a sacred value to human rights and effectively respected them, at least for their self-protection, Splatterkapitalismus grants no sacred value even to the lives of those in power. For the system, the boss is none other than a provisional functionary:

> The dictatorship of a man in the clan is always short-termed, if the power of one boss was to last too long, prices would rise and market monopolies arise, markets would become rigid and investment remain in the same markets rather than explore new ones (2006: 222).

Marx's description of the overall process of valorization started from the social cooperation where infinite atoms of abstract labor time combine. At the end of his investigation on the splatter-commodity, Saviano seeks a theoretical metaphor to describe this process with equal effectiveness, but it is a desperate attempt:

> The most complicated thing is imagining an economy in all of its parts. The financial flows, profit margins, debt negotiations, investments. There are no physiognomies that can be visualized, no precise elements to arise in the mind (2006: 310).

Then, in a genial logical leap he finally finds the most essential place of contemporary hyper capitalism: 'Waste grounds are the most concrete emblems of every economic cycle' (2006:310).

Hyper-capitalism continuously increases its productive capacity because it founds its power on it, not because there is any need for increasing production. There already is enough to feed six billion human beings on the planet; every year millions of tons of food are destroyed to avoid crises of overproduction. The clothes we use largely exceed our needs, and every other commodity is available in the countless warehouses that modern industry has furnished us with. So why are we accelerating so much, why are faster rhythms of labor implemented, why do we run more and more frenetically? Because hyper-capitalism is intimately Splatter.

Capitalism can only be described with the metaphor of cancer, which is not even a metaphor, but a clinically exact analysis. In the dumping grounds of Campania, cancer is badly disguised under a cliff, a light layer of rotten grass. Young Bocconi graduates provide the companies of Lombardy, Emilia and Germany with the lands in Campania where millions of cubic meters of cancerous substances can be damped.

> The region is engulfed in rubbish and finding solutions seems impossible (2006: 325).

Lands are ridden with dioxin. Fifteen year old kids sent by the camorra of the dumping ground to breath the air filled with death complete the operations of waste disposal.

> The more these young drivers heard people say that their activity was dangerous, the more they felt worthy of such important missions. None of them could think of themselves doing chemotherapy ten years later, or vomiting bile with rotten stomachs, livers and intestines (2006: 329).

The final pages of *Gomorra* describe scenery of fields poisoned by garbage, residues and rubbish. With a handkerchief around his mouth, trying to breath as little as possible, Saviano asks us what to do.

> Maybe we can only forget, or not see, and listen to the official version of events. I asked myself whether anything could make life happy, but maybe all I wanted was to stop dreaming about emancipation and anarchic freedoms, and throw myself into the arena, stick a semi automatic in my pants and start talking business, real business (2006: 330).

Hope

Is there still an answer to the question 'What is to be done?' Is there an answer, beyond the obvious advice to stop proliferating, to stop throwing innocent flesh onto the expanding burning stake? For the moment, there is no other answer.

But a new army raises from the four corners of the world, without flags, with no future, its only hope being suicide. The main discomfort of the participants to the recent Congress of the Chinese Communist Party was caused by the tens of thousands of peasants who kill themselves because economic growth drives them to leave the countryside and reduces them to conditions of hunger. The same occurs in India with the advancement of industrial modernization.

Since September 11th, 2001 suicide is the decisive political act of our times. When human life is worthless, humiliation grows until it becomes intolerable and explosive. Perhaps hope can only come from suicides.

3. The merchant, the warrior and the sage

On February 15th, 2003 when millions of people all over the world took to the streets to stop the war, many felt that military global power was about to lose all consensus and that this could signal the beginning of its crisis. But power is no longer grounded on consensus, but terror, ignorance and techno-economic financial and psychic automatisms that politics is no longer able to control and that mass action is no longer able to modify or stop.

In the following days we learned that a peace movement of gigantic proportions is not sufficient to stop war, and that democracy does not possess instruments capable of defusing military automatisms that terrorism and security paranoia have set in motion. Even if the majority of public opinion opposes war, the dynamic that leads to war is not stopped. Terror is the political investment on which the Bush administration placed all of its bets. There is no need to create consensus through discursive, propagandistic, and ideological instruments, it is sufficient to use psychic automatisms founded on terror. Terror is born before the terrorist attacks, terror is born out of the cruel and continuous competitiveness that the principle *mors tua vita mea* has inculcated into the mind of every individual.

The history of the twentieth century is the history of the conflict and alliances of three figures. The sage is the heir of human labor, the bearer of the intelligence accumulated by the infinite succession of acts of labor and the infinite series of acts of the refusal of labor. The refusal of labor induces the evolutive motion of intelligence. Intelligence is the refusal of work, actualized into a socially useful form. Because of intelligence it becomes possible to substitute human labor with machines. Because of the refusal of work, science is pushed forward, developed, put into practice. From the outset, modern science has been aware of its function in this respect.

Knowledge multiplies the human capacity to produce useful things and the spaces of freedom for all human beings, by reducing the necessary labor time to produce whatever society needs. This means that to know is to have power. The merchant and the warrior want to turn knowledge into an instrument of power. And to this end they have to subdue the sage. But this does not occur easily, because knowledge does not tolerate domination. Thus, the warrior and the merchant resort to traps and deceit, to submit the power of thinking to the power of money and violence.

The common interest of humanity

In a 1958 book entitled *Brighter than a Thousand Suns*, Robert Jungk tells of how in the Second World War the warrior captured the sage, through the history of the Manhattan project that led to the creation of the nuclear bomb. A group of scientists was faced with blackmail: Hitler might be preparing a nuclear bomb. We need to hurry, to anticipate him. According to Jungk:

In the Summer of 1939 twelve men, the physicists who were working on the Manhattan project, could have agreed to stop the construction of atomic bombs. But they missed their opportunity and were unable to decisively make their thoughts and actions adequate to the future consequences of scientific discoveries; neither did they have, in such critical situation, enough faith in the traditions of their profession. At the end of the war, von Weizsaecker commented, 'the fact that we were a family was not sufficient, maybe we should have been an international body with disciplinary powers over its members. But is such thing possible in modern science? (1958)

In Weizsaecker's words we find the problem that we encountered again in its full expression half a century later: which organizational form and what rules can those who produce knowledge give themselves, if we want to stop political, economic and military power from using knowledge for purposes that are extraneous to knowledge itself, and above all, contrary to the common interest of humanity? On that occasion, the US government managed to convince a group of scientists to surrender to its blackmail. The effect of the sage's surrender to the warrior was Hiroshima.

At that moment the struggle for the liberation of the sage from the warrior began, and it culminated in 1968. 1968 represented first of all the sage's refusal to lend her knowledge to the warrior and the decision to place the sage at the service of society. Then the merchant came along to seduce the sage and subdue her knowledge to the domination of techno-economic automatisms. The evaluation of the truth of knowledge is submitted to the criteria of competitiveness, economic efficiency, and the pursuit of maximum profit.

In the two decades inaugurated by Thatcher and Reagan, knowledge has been put to work in conditions of absolute dependence on capital. Science has been incorporated into the automatisms of technology, deprived of the possibility of changing the finalities that guide its functional operation. The intensive application of knowledge to production is concretized in the creation of the digital techno-sphere, which emanates effects of extraordinary power. But this power is submitted to the technical automatisms where power is articulated. Constrained within the categories of the profit economy, technology increases the productivity of labor while simultaneously multiplying misery, the subordination of human beings to wage labor, solitude, unhappiness and psychopathology.

I remember when I was a child in the 1950s, like everyone else I was fascinated by the idea that we would have lived the year 2000. Newspapers used to write that in the year 2000 all the problems of humanity would have been solved because technology would have assured peace, freedom and abundance. Now that the year 2000 has come, however, instead of peace, war hangs over the world as never before, atomic bombs proliferate in the hands of fanatics of all religions. Instead of freedom there is the unquestionable domination of economic priorities, instead of abundance there is slavery, misery and hunger in two thirds of the world. The fanatic application of market rules has produced this folly and we are racing towards catastrophe.

The movement of researchers

Any project of reform or change makes no sense unless we are prepared to radically redefine the direction of this race, and neither the warrior nor the merchant can decide the direction of the race. Only the sage can establish it. Only human knowledge, following its own rules, its priorities and lines of possibility has the right to redefine the rules of production and exchange. Only women and men as subjects of knowledge can decide in which direction the world is to move. This is the great novelty affirmed in Seattle: the merchants have no right to decide on the lives of millions of people on the basis of their own economic profit. Only a movement of researchers, a high tech labor movement of the cognitariat that is autonomously organized can stop the dictatorship of financial corporations. The global movement that exploded in Seattle in 1999 pointed towards a new direction: globalization must be guided by ethically motivated knowledge and become a power in the hands of all women and men, not the power of a minority.

From Seattle onwards a movement emerged that aims at the social, epistemic and technological recomposition of cognitive labor. This requires that scientific research is autonomous from the merchants' interests. This awareness has grown ever since: millions of people in the world have started to reclaim the autonomy of their brain from profit. In information technology we have witnessed the diffusion of open source practices; in biotechnological and pharmacological sectors there has been a struggle to claim free access to the products of intellectual innovation; in the cycle of information media activism has spread.

The privatization of knowledge

Capital reacted, following the dictates of liberalist ideology, with the coercive privatization of the products of collective knowledge and the submission of experimentation to economic competition. The privatization of collective knowledge has encountered resistance and opposition everywhere, and cognitive laborers have started to realize that their potential is superior to the power of the merchant. Since intellectual labor is at the center of the productive scene, the merchant no longer possesses the juridical or material instruments to impose the principle of private property. Given that the most precious goods in social production have an immaterial and reproducible character, we have discovered that the private appropriation of goods makes no sense, while the reasons sustaining the privatization of material goods in industrial society have weakened. In the sphere of semiotic-capital and cognitive labor, when a product is consumed, instead of disappearing it remains available, while its value increases the more its use is shared. This is how the network economy works, and this contradicts the very principle of private property on which capitalism was founded until now.

Since this perspective has started to spread, the warrior has come back on the scene, with the old economy of petrol magnates and arms producers. The amount of sadness, fear and anxiety accumulated in the folds of social labor during the 1990s has now been turned into fanaticism, aggressiveness and obsession with identity. The merchant has resorted to the warrior to submit the sage again. Bill Gates allied himself with George Bush. The merchant who robbed collective intelligence allied himself with the idiot warrior and together they try to suffocate any inch of wisdom, to subsume once and for all knowledge to profit and power.

Thanks to the opening of the stock market to the masses carried out in the 1990s, a mass participation with the profit of capital was possible and this resulted in the dotcom economy. This also opened the possibility for a vast process of self-organization of cognitive laborers. Cognitive laborers invested their competence, knowledge and creativity and found the means to create an enterprise in the stock market. For several years the form of enterprise was the point of encounter for financial capital and cognitive labor at a high productivity rate. A new form of self-enterprise glorified at once the autonomy of labor and the dependency on the market.

After a decade of uninterrupted growth and social alliance between cognitive labor and recombining capital, this alliance was broken. The fall of the stock market that began in April 2000 was the beginning of a political crisis of the relation of capital and cognitive labor. Many different factors provoked this rupture. First of all, the collapse of the psychic and social energies of cognitive labor: overexploitation, the acceleration of life rhythms, the twenty four hour long working day of mobile phone workers, depression, the excessive use of stimulant drugs to sustain the pace of hyper-labor have lead the cognitive laborer into a depressive phase. The collapse came from inside. At the same time, the monopolistic attack against the army of dotcom, the front of cognitive laborers and the free market occurred. The imposition of limits on experimentation, the imposition of monopolistic standards, the alliance between monopolies and political power, took the breath away from the diffuse economy. Then the monopolistic counterrevolution began and the conditions for a shift from the network economy to the war economy were created.

The new economy had witnessed the flourishing of a process of self-organization of cognitive labor in the form of the enterprise, but in the same years a predatory lumpenbourgeoisie emerged to take advantage of the crisis of traditional capitalist rule in order to appropriate for itself enormous shares of social capital, as all the post-Enron collapse cases demonstrated. Neoliberalism in the long run has not favored the free market but monopoly.

At this stage, almost miraculously, while the crisis precipitated and was taking away all credibility and power of the groups linked to the Bush administration, those airplanes fell from the sky and gave birth to an era of unlimited violence, an era when power, having lost all legitimacy, legitimates itself through war. But in war, perspectives are redefined. Nazi-liberal aggressive capitalism evoked the specter of the war to defend its vacillating power, but in the course of this war, which is unacceptable for the conscience and lifestyle of the great majority of the western population, anything could happen.

The problem Weizsaecker talks about is urgent today: is it possible to have a self-organization of scientists that is founded on the autonomy of science from power? This is no longer a concern for a small group of nuclear physicists, but for millions and millions of workers in science and technology, in administration, in education and therapy.

The pacific army of the cognitariat holds the key to a deconstruction of the chain of automatisms through which capitalism fortifies itself.

From intellectuals to cognitarians

The Enlightenment intellectual is defined not by his social condition, but by a universal system of values. The role that the Enlightenment attributes to the intellectual is that of founding and guaranteeing, through the exercise of rationality, the realization of universal principles such as respect for the rights of man, equality before the law, and the universality of law itself. This modern figure of the intellectual – one that incarnates an ideology – finds its philosophical legitimation in Kantian thought. In the context of Kantian thought the intellectual emerges as a transcendent figure whose activity is independent of social experience, or in any case not socially determined in its cognitive or ethical decisions. The intellectual appears in the Enlightenment era as the bearer of a universal rationality, abstractly human, and in this sense one can consider him as the subjective determination of the Kantian 'I think.'

The role of the intellectual is closely tied to the elaboration of that system of values constituting modern universalism. The intellectual is the guarantor of a thought free from any belonging, an expression of a universally human rationality. In this sense, the intellectual is the guarantor of democracy. Such a democracy cannot descend from social origins, from a belonging, but only from the desert, from the unlimited horizon of choice and of possibilities, from the possibility of access and of citizenship for every person as semiotic agent, a subject that exchanges signs in order to access universal rationality. This detached, universal intellectual is established in opposition to the romantic figure of 'the people,' or rather withdraws itself from it. Universal thought, from which the modern adventure of democracy is born, evades the territoriality of culture. Democracy cannot carry the imprint of a culture, of a people, of a tradition; it must be a game without foundation, invention and convention, not the affirmation of a belonging.

Significantly different is the point of view of the revolutionary intellectual that is linked to and affirms itself by way of historical-dialectical thought. In the Eleventh Thesis on Feuerbach, Marx refers to the role that knowledge must play in the historical process: "Philosophers have hitherto only interpreted the world in various ways; the point is to change it." The Marxist intellectual is an instrument of the historical process of achieving a classless society. With Marx thought becomes historically effective only when it recognizes in the working class the horizon of action. The communist project gives theory a material potency and makes knowledge an instrument for changing the world. Only inasmuch as he participates in the struggle for the abolition of class and of waged labor, does the intellectual become the bearer of a universal mission. In this vision the intellectual has nothing to do with the people (*Volk*), because the people is the territorialized figure of belonging, the predominance of *Kultur* with respect to reason, the preeminence of the root with respect to finality. On the contrary, the working class does not belong to any territory, culture, or lineage, and its mental horizon is that of a universally exploited class, striving towards a universal task of liberation from exploitation.

From the organic intellectual to the General Intellect

The role of intellectuals is central in the political philosophy of the twentieth century, and particularly in communist revolutionary thought. In *What is to be Done?*, Lenin asks himself how it is possible to organize collective action, and how the activity of intellectuals can become effective. For Lenin intellectuals are not a social class; they have no specific social interests to uphold. They are generally an expression of parasitic profit and can make 'purely intellectual' choices, turning themselves into intermediaries and organizers of a revolutionary consciousness descending from philosophical thought. In this sense intellectuals are very similar to the pure becoming of the 'spirit,' to the Hegelian unfolding of self-consciousness. On the other hand, the workers, still bearers of social interests, can only pass from a purely economic phase (the Hegelian 'in itself' of the social being) to a politically conscious phase (the 'for itself' of self-consciousness) through the political form of the party, which incarnates and transmits a philosophical legacy. Marx speaks of the proletariat as heir to German classical philosophy: thanks to workers' struggles a historical realization of the dialectical horizon becomes possible – the arrival of the end-point of German philosophical development from Kantian Enlightenment to romantic idealism.

In Gramsci the reflection on intellectuals connotes social analysis, and approaches a materialist formulation of the 'organic' relationship between intellectuals and the working class. Nonetheless, the collective dimension of intellectual activity remains within the party, defined as the collective intellectual. The intellectual of the Gramscian tradition (the one that has yet to be put to work by the digital network) therefore cannot access the collective and political dimension except through the party. But in the second part of the twentieth century, following mass education and the techno-scientific transformation of production which came about through the direct integration of different knowledges, the role of intellectuals was redefined. No longer are intellectuals a class independent of production, or free individualities that take upon themselves the task of a purely ethical and freely cognitive choice; instead the intellectual becomes a mass social subject that tends to become an integral part of the general productive process. Paolo Virno uses the term 'mass intellectuality' to denote the formation of social subjectivity tied to the mass standardization of intellectual capacity in advanced industrial society.

The birth of the student movement in the 1960s was the sign of the mutation of the social scenario out of which emerges this new figure of mass intellectuality. The student movement became a decisive actor of modern history when, in 1968, the social effects of mass schooling came into their maturity. For the first time in history the intellectual function recognized itself as a mass political subject. The student movement possessed only a partial consciousness of the social mutation it was signaling. In Europe at least a hefty part of the student movement tried to interpret its own role according to the categories of Marxist-Leninism, conceiving of itself as a political vanguard, an army of intellectuals at the service of the people. But in the very same movement of intellectual labor in formation there emerged the prospect of the social organization of mass intellectuality. Hans Jürgen Krahl, a leader of the German student movement, shortly before his untimely death in a car accident, wrote the *Theses on Techno-Scientific Intelligence* which were published in the journal *Sozialistische Korrespondenz* – Info 25, in 1969, and then in the book *Konstitution und Klassenkampf* (1969). Krahl states for the first time that the new social composition of intellectualized labor cannot be organized according to the political and organizational categories of the traditional worker's movement.

Preceding and in parallel with the movements of 1968, Italian operaismo brought to light, in an original manner through its analytic approach, this necessary inversion of perspective at the end of the 1960s (Mario Tronti, Raniero Panzieri, Toni Negri, Romano Alquati). I prefer to speak of this stream of thought as 'compositionism,' due to the fact that its essential theoretical contribution consists in the reformulation of the problem of political organization in terms of social composition. Compositionism abandons the Leninist notion of the Party as collective intellectual and leaves open the notion of the intellectual itself, by proposing a re-examination of the Marxian concept of 'General Intellect.'

Marx spoke of the General Intellect in a section of the *Grundrisse* known as the "Fragment on Machines":

> But to the degree that large industry develops, the creation of real wealth comes to depend less on labor time and on the amount of labor employed than on the power of the agencies set in motion during labor time, whose 'powerful effectiveness' is itself in turn out of all proportion to the direct labor time spent on their production, but depends rather on the general state of science and on the progress of technology, or the application of science to production... Real wealth manifests itself, rather – and large industry reveals this – in the monstrous disproportion between labor time applied, and its product, as well as in the qualitative imbalance between labor, reduced to a pure abstraction, and the power of the production process it superintends.

> Nature builds no machines, no locomotives, railways, electric telegraphs, self-acting mules, etc. These are products of human industry; natural material transformed into the organs of the human will over nature, or of human participation in nature.

They are organs of the human brain, created by the human hand; the power of knowledge, objectified. The development of fixed capital indicates to what degree social knowledge has become a direct force of production, and to what degree, hence, the conditions of the process of social life itself have come under the control of the General Intellect and been transformed in accordance with it. To what degree powers of social production have been produced, not only in the form of knowledge, but also as immediate organs of social practice, of the real life process (1973: 704-706).

During the century of communist revolutions, the Marxist-Leninist tradition disregarded and relegated to the background the notion of the General Intellect, even though in the post-industrial productive transformation it emerged as a central productive force. At the end of the century, thanks to digital technologies and the creation of the global telematic network, the general social process is redefined by the General Intellect and the Leninist conception of the party definitively abandons the stage. Even the Gramscian notion of the organic intellectual loses coherence since it is based on the adherence of intellectuals to an ideology, while what counts now is the formation of a new social concatenation, which we can call the cognitariat, representing the social subjectivity of the General Intellect.

The cognitariat and recombination

If we want to define the 'what is to be done' of our times we need to concentrate our attention on the social function of cognitive labor. It is no longer a case of constructing a vanguard-subjectivity – the organic intellectual – to organize the collective intellectual in the party; rather, it is a matter of creating *movements* capable of organizing cognitive laborers as a factor of transformation for the entire cycle of social labor. The problem of our time is the creation of a *recombinant function*, a function of subjectivity capable of spanning the various domains of social production, and recombining them within a paradigmatic frame that is not dependent on profit but upon social utility.

No longer a social function separated from general labor, intellectual labor becomes a function transversal to the entire social process. It is in fact the creation of techno-linguistic interfaces that allows the fluidity of the process and its recombinant power [*potere*]. *Recombining* does not mean to subvert or to overthrow, nor to bring to the surface a hidden social authenticity, but rather means assembling elements of knowledge according to criteria other than those of profit and the accumulation of value. It is no longer a case of constructing forms of political representation but of giving form to processes of knowledge, and of technical and productive concatenation based on epistemological models that are autonomous of profit and instead motivated by their social utility. Intellectuals no longer find the realm of political action to be outside of their daily practices; it now lies in the transversal connections between knowledge and social practices.

The programmer must be a programmer, the doctor must be a doctor, the bioengineer must be a bioengineer, and the architect must be an architect. Under the Leninist vision though, each of them must be a revolutionary by vocation, because this means bringing revolutionary consciousness to workers from the exterior. Yet in today's context, in the first place, the programmer, the engineer, the doctor, and the architect must reorient their cognitive action, modifying the structure and function of their specific field of knowledge and of their field of productive action.

The analytic separation between the economic sphere and consciousness enjoyed an actual foundation when productive labor was structurally separate from intellectual labor; yet the meaning of such a division is lost the moment intellectual labor is subsumed by the broader process of production. Production is not to be considered as a purely economic process, governed exclusively by laws of exchange; extraeconomic factors enter into that process and reveal themselves to be all the more decisive when the labor cycle is intellectualized. Social culture, contrasting imaginations, expectations and disappointments, loathing and solitude enter to modify the rhythm and fluidity of the productive process. Social productivity is conditioned by the emotional, ideological and linguistic spheres. And this becomes all the more clear as emotional, linguistic, and planning spheres become involved to a greater degree in the process of the production of value.

Social combination gives production an ever-greater scientific character, and, in this way, forms it into a totality, a general laborer, but at the same time it reduces the single capacity for labor to a simple moment of production. The application of science and technique to the productive process has reached such a level of development that it threatens to unravel the system. It therefore has induced a new quality of the socialization of productive labor which no longer tolerates the form of objectification imposed on labor by capital (Krahl 1969: 365).

On the basis of these premises Krahl critiques the political planning of the twentieth century labor movement:

The absence of reflection on the professional constitution (*Verfassung*) of class-consciousness as a non-empirical category has introduced into the socialist movement a tacit reduction of class consciousness in a Leninist sense that is inadequate to the metropolis (1969: 367).

Leninism, then, is inadequate both as an organizational model and as a conception of the relationship between social consciousness and the broader labor process, with respect to the metropolitan condition. We might add that Leninism is completely inadequate when the social composition of labor assumes the form of a network. The Leninist view was founded on a separation between the labor process and cognitive activity of a superior kind (let's call it consciousness). This separation has a basis in the proto-industrial form of labor, in which the worker possesses knowledge of his or her trade but does not possess any knowledge of the system of knowledge that structures society. But the basis of that separation becomes increasingly fragile at the moment in which the mass-worker, forced into an ever more fragmented and repetitive labor activity, develops his sociality in a dimension that is immediately subversive and anticapitalist. And finally that separation no longer has any basis when we deal with mental labor, when single intellectualized workers become the bearers of a specific consciousness and of an awareness, although tormented, uneven, and fragmentary, of the social system of knowledge that spans the entirety of its productive cycles.

All of this was made abundantly clear during dotcom-mania in the 1990s, which made possible a vast process of self-organization of cognitive producers; they were able to invest their competencies, knowledge and creativity, finding in the stock market the means to finance their desire for achievement. But dotcom-mania was dominated by a somewhat fanatic ideology of liberal optimism that made cognitive laborers subordinate to the domain of finance capital. Yet the real process that unfolded in the dotcom years contained elements of social as well as technological innovation. In the second half of the 1990s a veritable class struggle took place within the productive circuits of high technology. The becoming of the network was marked by this struggle. The monopolies in software, telecommunications, entertainment, and advertising took advantage of the labor of collective intelligence, and are now attempting to take away its tools of self-organization in order to force it into a condition of flexible, precarious, and cellularized subjection. The dotcoms were a laboratory for the formation of a productive model, and of a market. In the end the market was captured and suffocated by monopolies which the army of self-entrepreneurs and venture micro-capitalists robbed and dissolved. In this way a new phase began: the monopolistic groups that gained the upper hand within the cycle of the net-economy ally themselves with the dominant group from the old economy (the Bush clan, representatives of oil and of the military), and this marks a blockage of a particular project of globalization. Neoliberalism has produced its own negation: monopolistic domination and state-military dictatorship. Cognitive laborers, who were enthusiastic supporters of liberal ideology, became its marginalized victims.

The promise implicit in the ideology of the new economy was that of high compensation and participation in the economic fortunes of the system. But by 2000, the new economy house of cards collapsed, and a crisis of the virtual class commenced. The psychic energy invested in the economy dissipated. The possibilities of obtaining high compensation, or even meaningful employment diminished in the innovative sectors, and this insecurity currently risks turning into panic.

The mutation of this scenario was to produce a transformation in the recombinant prospects of the cycle of cognitive labor. The virtual class, sure of itself, enclosed in the circuits of an economy that believed itself to be impermeable to the adversities of the material world and sheltered from cyclical crises, is now forced to recognize itself as cognitariat, a proletariat endowed with extraordinary intellectual means, a repository of the knowledge upon which capitalist society rests. The happy yuppie discovers that he is an exploited worker, and it is in this discovery that there lies the condition for a process of self-organization of cognitive labor. The figure of the intellectual emerges completely redefined by the evolutions which verified themselves in production in recent decades.

The cognitariat against capitalist cybertime

Rosa Luxemburg believed that capitalism is inherently pushed towards a process of continual expansion. Imperialism is the political, economic, and military expression of this need for continual expansion that brings capital to continually extend its domain.

But what happens when every space of the planetary territory has been subjected to the power [*potere*] of the capitalist economy and every object of daily life has been transformed into a commodity? In late modernity capitalism seems to have exhausted every possibility for further expansion. For a certain period the conquest of extraterrestrial space seemed to be a new direction of development for capitalist expansion. Subsequently we saw that the direction of development is above all the conquest of internal space, the interior world, the space of the mind, of the soul, the space of time.

The colonization of time has been a fundamental objective of the development of capitalism during the modern era: the anthropological mutation which capitalism produced in the human mind and in daily life has been above all a transformation in the perception of time. Yet with the spread of digital technologies, which allow absolute acceleration, something new occurs. Time becomes the primary battlefield, as it is the space of the mind: mind-time, cybertime. Thus we must introduce a distinction between the concept of *cyberspace* and the concept of *cybertime*. This distinction is key to the contemporary techno-subjective arrangement of struggle. The *potenza* of this new figure of intellectuality of the 'cognitariat' is being reterritorialized by way of the tyrannical operation of capitalist cybertime.

Cyberspace is the sphere of connection of innumerable human and machinic sources of enunciation, the sphere of connection between minds and machines in unlimited expansion. This sphere can grow indefinitely, because it is the point of intersection between the organic body and the inorganic body of the electronic machine. But cyberspace is not the only dimension possible for the development of this interconnection: the other side of the process is cybertime. This is the organic side of the process, and its expansion is limited by organic factors. The human brain's capacity to elaborate can be expanded with drugs, with training and attention, thanks to the expansion of intellectual capacity, but it has limits of time, connected to the emotional, sensitive dimension of the conscious organism.

Generally we call cyberspace the global universe of the infinite possible relations of a rhizomatic system which virtually connects every human terminal with every other human terminal, and which simultaneously connects human and machinic terminals. Cyberspace is a neuro-telematic rhizome, therefore a non-hierarchical and non-linear network connecting human minds and electronic devices. Cybertime, on the contrary, is not a purely extendable dimension, because it is connected with the intensity of experience that the conscious organism dedicates to the elaboration of information coming from cyberspace.

The objective sphere of cyberspace expands at the speed of digital replication, but the subjective nucleus of cybertime evolves at a slower rhythm, the rhythm of 'corporeality,' that of pleasure and suffering. Thus as the technical composition of the world changes, cognitive appropriation and psychic responsiveness do not follow in a linear manner. The mutation of the technological environment is much more rapid than the changes in cultural habits and cognitive models.

As the stratum of the info-sphere becomes progressively denser, the informational stimuli invade every atom of human attention. Cyberspace grows in an unlimited fashion, yet mental time is not infinite. The subjective nucleus of cybertime follows the slow rhythm of organic matter. We can increase the time of exposure of the organism to information, but experience cannot be intensified beyond certain limits.

Beyond these limits, the acceleration of experience provokes a reduced consciousness of stimulus, a loss of intensity which concerns the aesthetic sphere, that of sensibility, and importantly also the sphere of ethics. The experience of the other is rendered banal; the other becomes part of an uninterrupted and frenetic stimulus, and loses its singularity and intensity – it loses its beauty.

Thus we have less curiosity, less surprise; more stress, aggressiveness, anxiety, and fear. The acceleration produces an impoverishment of experience, because we are exposed to a growing mass of stimuli that we cannot elaborate upon, according to the intensive modalities of pleasure and knowledge.

Again, we have more information, less meaning; more information, less pleasure. Sensibility is within time. Sensuality is in slowness, and the space of information is too vast and fast to elaborate upon it intensively, deeply. At the point of intersection between electronic cyberspace and organic cybertime is found the fundamental crux of the present mutation. The great majority of humanity is subjected to the invasion of the video-electronic flux, and suffers the superimposition of digital code over the codes of recognition and of identification of reality that permeate organic cultures.

The psychopathic epidemic that appears to be spreading in social behaviors also depends on this gap, on this asymmetry between the format of emission (the techno-communicative system) and the format of reception (the social mind). The acceleration produced by network technologies and the condition of precariousness and dependence of cognitive labor, forced as it is to be subject to the pace of the productive network, has produced a saturation of human attention which has reached pathological levels.

In the labor process we no longer have availability of time; attention is supersaturated. First of all we have no time for attention within work, and secondly we have no time for affect, for that kind of spatial attention that is eroticism, the attention to our body and to that of others. Sensibility tends to become obtuse. But what happens when we no longer have the time for attention?

What happens is that we perceive things badly; we are no longer able to make decisions in a rational manner. This is producing an effect that psychiatrists define as panic. Society risks being propelled into a condition of panic, of diffuse psychopathology, of desensitization and disaffection. Annoyance in the face of the other and the aggressive reaction are the roots of the new climate of war into which the West has fallen.

To understand the origin of this social psychopathology we must first look at the relationship between cyberspace and cybertime. *Cyberspace is the infinite productivity of the general intelligence, of the General Intellect, of the net.* When an immense number of points enter into a non-centric and non-hierarchical connection we have the infinite production of signs, i.e. intellectual commodities.

Yet cybertime is by no means infinite. *Cybertime is the organic, physical, finite capacity to elaborate information.* This ability is found in our mind, and our mind needs slowness in elaboration time, it needs to affectively singularize information. If elaboration time disappears the human mind is forced to follow the rhythm of the machinic network, and this brings about a pathology that manifests itself as panic and as depression on an individual level, and as generalized aggressiveness on a collective scale.

One answer to 'what is to be done?' is that the intellectual, and thus radical pedagogy, must learn from this gap between cyberspace and cybertime. It is only by freeing the cognitariat from the subordination to its virtual dimension, it is only by reactivating a dynamic of slow affectivity, of freedom from work, that the collective organism will be able to regain its sensibility and rationality, its ability to live in peace.

The cognitariat versus war economy

Only the autonomy of science from power can deconstruct the chain of automatisms in which capitalism fortressed itself. This is no longer a concern for a small group of nuclear physicists, but for millions and millions of workers in science and technology, in administration, in education and therapy.

I do not think that freeware and open source are outside the sphere of capitalism. Similarly I do not think that the worker's collective strike and self-organization in the old Fordist factory was outside the sphere of capitalism. Nothing is outside the sphere of capitalism, because capitalism is not a dialectical totality suited to being overcome (*Aufgeheben*) by a new totality like communism, or something like that. Capital is a cognitive framework of social activity, a semiotic frame embedded in the social psyche and in the human techne. Refusal of work, temporary autonomous zones, open source and freeware, all this is not the new totality, it is the dynamic recombination allowing people to find their space of autonomy, and push capitalism towards progressive innovation.

The danger in the process of the transmission of knowledge is the following: the 'power point' technicalities creating the 'Novum Organum' of science. Knowledge reduced to a functional system of frequently asked questions, the digital formalization of didactics, of the method and of the contents of knowledge. You will remember that Karl Marx wrote somewhere that the proletariat is the heir of classical German philosophy. It was just a metaphor. But now we can say in a strictly literal sense that the cognitariat is the heir of modern science and philosophy, and also the heir of modern art and poetry. The social liberation of the cognitariat is also their appropriation of the techno-social effects of knowledge.

Intellectuals, cognitarians and social composition

Following the Leninist tradition, the party used to be the professional organization of intellectuals who chose to serve the proletarian cause. Antonio Gramsci introduced decisive elements of innovation to the Leninist conception, because he introduced the theme of cultural hegemony, of the specificity of ideology to the development of the process of seizing political power. But Gramsci remained fundamentally attached to an idea of the intellectual as an unproductive figure, to an idea of culture as pure consensus with ideological values. The industrialization of culture that developed during the 1900s modified these figures, and critical thought realized this when it migrated from Frankfurt to Hollywood. Benjamin and Marcuse, Adorno and Horkheimer, Brecht and Krakauer registered this passage. But when the digital web fragmented and recombined the global labor process, then intellectual labor assumed the configuration that Marx had, in the *Grundrisse*, defined with the expression of 'General Intellect.'

Pierre Levy calls it collective intelligence, Derrick De Kerkhove points out that it actually is a connective intelligence. The infinitely fragmented mosaic of cognitive labor becomes a fluid process within a universal telematic network, and thus the shape of labor and capital are redefined. Capital becomes the generalized semiotic flux that runs through the veins of the global economy, while labor becomes the constant activation of the intelligence of countless semiotic agents linked to one another.

Retrieving the concept of 'General Intellect' in the 1990s, Italian compositionist thought led by Paolo Virno, Christian Marazzi, Carlo Formenti and Maurizio Lazzarato, has introduced the concept of mass intellectuality, and emphasized the interaction between labor and language.

4. What is the meaning of autonomy today?

I do not intend to give a historical account of the movement called *Autonomia*, but I want to understand its peculiarity through an overview of some concepts like refusal of work, and class composition. Journalists often use the word 'Operaismo' to define a political and philosophical movement which surfaced in Italy during the 1960s. I dislike this term absolutely, because it reduces the complexity of social reality to the mere datum of the centrality of the industrial workers in the social dynamics of late modernity.

The origin of this philosophical and political movement can be identified in the works of Mario Tronti, Romano Alquati, Raniero Panzieri, and Toni Negri, and its central focus can be seen in the emancipation from the Hegelian concept of subject.

In place of the historical subject inherited from the Hegelian legacy, we should speak of the process of becoming subject. Subjectivation takes the conceptual place of subject. This conceptual move is very close to the contemporary modification of the philosophical landscape that was promoted by French post-structuralism. Subjectivation in the place of subject. That means that we should not focus on identity, but on the process of becoming. This also means that the concept of social class is not to be seen as an ontological concept, but rather as a vectorial concept.

In the framework of autonomous thought the concept of social class is redefined as an investment of social desire, and that means culture, sexuality, refusal of work. In the 1960s and 1970s the thinkers who wrote in magazines like *Classe Operaia*, and *Potere Operaio* did not speak of social investments of desire: they spoke in a much more Leninist way. But their philosophical gesture produced an important change in the philosophical landscape, from the centrality of the worker identity to the decentralization of the process of subjectivation.

Félix Guattari has always emphasized the idea that we should not talk of subject, but of 'processus de subjectivation.' From this perspective we can understand what the expression refusal of work means.

Refusal of work does not mean so much the obvious fact that workers do not like to be exploited, but something more. It means that capitalist restructuring, technological change, and the general transformation of social institutions are produced by the daily action of withdrawal from exploitation, of the rejection of the obligation to produce surplus value and to increase the value of capital by reducing the value of life. I do not like the term 'Operaismo', because of the implicit reduction to a narrow social reference (the workers, 'operai' in Italian), and I would prefer to use the word 'compositionism' The concept of social composition, or 'class composition' (widely used by the group of thinkers we are talking about), has much more to do with chemistry than with the history of society.

I like this idea that the place where social phenomena occur is not the solid, rocky historical territory of Hegelian descent, but a chemical environment where culture, sexuality, disease, and desire fight and meet and mix and continuously change the landscape. If we use the concept of composition, we can better understand what happened in Italy in the 1970s, and we can better understand what autonomy means: not the constitution of a subject, not the strong identification of human beings with a social destiny, but the continuous change of social relationships, sexual identification and de-identification, and the refusal of work. Refusal of work is actually generated by the complexity of social investments of desire.

In this view autonomy means that social life does not depend only on the disciplinary regulation imposed by economic power, but also depends on the internal displacement, shifts, settlings and dissolutions that are the process of the self-composition of living society; struggle, withdrawal, alienation, sabotage, and lines of flight from the capitalist system of domination.

Autonomy is the independence of social time from the temporality of capitalism.

This is the meaning of the expression refusal of work. It means quite simply: I don't want to go to work because I prefer to sleep. But this laziness is the source of intelligence, of technology, of progress. Autonomy is the self-regulation of the social body in its independence and in its interaction with the disciplinary norm.

There is another side of autonomy, which has been scarcely

recognized so far. The process of the becoming autonomous of workers away from their disciplinary role has provoked a social earthquake which triggered capitalist deregulation. The deregulation that entered the world scene in the Thatcher-Reagan era, can be seen as the capitalist response to the autonomization from the disciplinary order of labor. Workers demanded freedom from capitalist regulation, then capital did the same thing, but in a reverse way. Freedom from state regulation has become economic despotism over the social fabric. Workers demanded freedom from the life-time prison of the industrial factory. Deregulation responded with the flexibilization and the fractalization of labor.

The autonomy movement of the 1970s triggered a dangerous process, a process which evolved from the social refusal of capitalist disciplinary rule to capitalist revenge, which took the form of deregulation, freedom of the enterprise from the state, destruction of social protections, downsizing and externalization of production, cutback of social spending, de-taxation, and finally flexibilization.

The movement of autonomization did, in fact, trigger the destabilization of the social framework resulting from a century of pressure on the part of the unions and of state regulation. Was it a terrible mistake that we made? Should we repent the actions of sabotage and dissent, of autonomy, of refusal of work which seem to have provoked capitalist deregulation? Absolutely not.

The movement of autonomy actually forestalled the capitalist move, but the process of deregulation was inscribed in the coming capitalist post-industrial development and was naturally implied in the technological restructuring and in the globalization of production.

There is a close relationship between refusal of work, informatization of the factories, downsizing, outsourcing of jobs, and the flexibilization of labor. But this relationship is much more complex than a cause-and-effect chain. The process of deregulation was inscribed in the development of new technologies allowing capitalist corporations to unleash a process of globalization. A similar process happened in the media-field, during the same period.

Think about the free radio stations in the 1970s. In Italy at that time there was a state owned monopoly, and free broadcasting was forbidden. In 1975-76 a group of media activists began to create small free radio stations like Radio Alice in Bologna. The traditional left (the PCI and so on) denounced those media-activists, warning about the danger of weakening the public media system, and opening the door to privately owned media. Should we think today that those people of the traditional statist left were right? I don't think so, I think they were wrong at that time, because the end of the state-owned monopoly was inevitable, and freedom of expression is better than centralized media. The traditional statist left was a conservative force, doomed to defeat as they desperately tried to preserve an old framework which could no longer last in the new technological and cultural situation of the post-industrial transition.

We could say much the same about the end of the Soviet Empire and of so-called 'real socialism.'

Everybody knows that Russian people were probably living better twenty years ago than today, and the ostensible democratization of Russian society has so far mostly been the destruction of social protections, and the unleashing of a social nightmare of aggressive competition, violence, and economic corruption. But the dissolution of the socialist regime was inevitable, because that order was blocking the dynamic of the social investment of desire, and because the totalitarian regime was obstructing cultural innovation. The dissolution of the communist regimes was inscribed in the social composition of collective intelligence, in the imagination created by the new global media, and in the collective investment of desire. This is why the democratic intelligentsia and dissident cultural forces took part in the struggle against the socialist regime, although they knew that capitalism was not paradise. Now deregulation is savaging the former Soviet society, and people are experiencing exploitation and misery and humiliation at a point never reached before, but this transition was inevitable and in a sense it has to be seen as a progressive change. Deregulation does not mean only the emancipation of private enterprise from state regulation and a reduction of public spending and social protection. It also means an increasing flexibility of labor.

The reality of labor flexibility is the other side of this kind of emancipation from capitalist regulation. We should not underestimate the connection between refusal of work and the flexibilization which ensued.

I remember that one of the strong ideas of the movement of autonomous proletarians during the 1970s was the idea 'precariousness is good.' Job precariousness is a form of autonomy from steady regular work, lasting an entire life. In the 1970s many people used to work for a few months, then to go away for a journey, then back to work for a while. This was possible in times of almost full employment and in times of egalitarian culture. This situation allowed people to work in their own interest and not in the interest of capitalists, but quite obviously this could not last forever, and the neoliberal offensive of the 1980s was aimed to reverse this balance of forces.

Deregulation and the flexibilization of labor have been the effect and the reversal of the worker's autonomy and it is not only for historical reasons that we should try to grasp this. If we want to understand what has to be done today, in the age of fully flexibilized labor, we have to understand how the capitalist takeover of social desire could happen.

Cognitive labor and recombinant capital

During the last decades, the informatization of machinery has played a crucial role in making labor flexible, fostering the immateriality of production.

The introduction of the new electronic technologies into the production cycle, opened the way for the creation of a global network of info-production, deterritorialized, delocalized, depersonalized. The subject of work can be increasingly identified with the global network of info-production.

The industrial workers had been refusing their role in the factory and gaining freedom from capitalist domination. However, this situation drove the capitalists to invest in labor saving technologies and also to change the technical composition of the work process, in order to expel the well organized industrial workers and to create a new organization of labor which could be more flexible.

The increasing intellectual and immaterial nature of labor is one side of the social change in production forms. Planetary globalization is the other face. Immateriality and globalization are subsidiary and complementary. Globalization does indeed have a material side, because industrial labor does not disappear in the post-industrial age, but migrates towards the geographic zones where it is possible to pay low wages and regulations are poorly implemented.

In the last issue of the magazine *Classe Operaia* in 1967, Mario Tronti wrote: the most important phenomenon of the next decades will be the development of the working class on a global planetary scale. This intuition was not based on an analysis of the capitalist process of production, but rather on an understanding of the transformation in the social composition of labor. Globalization and informatization could be foretold as an effect of the refusal of work in the western capitalist countries.

During the last two decades of the twentieth century we have witnessed a sort of alliance between recombinant capital and cognitive work. What I call recombinant are those sections of capitalism which are not closely connected to a particular industrial application, but can be easily transferred from one place to another, from one industrial application to another, from one sector of economic activity to another and so on. The financial capital that takes the central role in politics and in the culture of the 1990s may be called recombinant. The alliance of cognitive labor and financial capital has produced important cultural effects, namely the ideological identification of labor and enterprise. The workers have been induced to see themselves as self-entrepreneurs, and this was not completely false in the dotcom period, when the cognitive worker could create his own enterprise, just investing his intellectual force (an idea, a project, a formula) as an asset. This was the period that Geert Lovink has defined as 'dotcommania' in his remarkable book *Dark Fiber* (2003).

What was dotcommania? Due to mass participation in the cycle of financial investment in the 1990s, a vast process of self-organization of cognitive producers got under way. Cognitive workers invested their expertise, their knowledge and their creativity, and found in the stock market the means to create enterprises. For several years, the entrepreneurial form became the point where financial capital and highly productive cognitive labor met. The libertarian and liberal ideology that dominated the (American) cyberculture of the 1990s idealized the market by presenting it as a pure environment. In this environment, as natural as the struggle for the survival of the fittest that makes evolution possible, labor would find the necessary means to valorize itself and become enterprise. Once left to its own dynamic, the reticular economic system was destined to optimize economic gains for everyone, owners and workers, also because the distinction between owners and workers would become increasingly imperceptible when one enters the virtual productive cycle. This model, theorized by authors such as Kevin Kelly and transformed by *Wired* magazine into a sort of digital liberal, scornful and triumphalist Weltanschauung, went bankrupt in the first couple of years of the new millennium, together with the new economy and a large part of the army of self-employed cognitive entrepreneurs who had inhabited the dotcom world. It went bankrupt because the model of a perfectly free market is a practical and theoretical lie. What neoliberalism supported in the long run was not the free market, but monopoly. While the market was idealized as a free space where knowledges, expertise and creativity meet, reality showed that the big groups of command operate in a way that is far from being libertarian, but instead introduces technological automatisms, imposing itself with the power of the media or money, and finally shamelessly robbing the mass of share holders and cognitive labor.

In the second half of the 1990s a real class struggle occurred within the productive circuit of high technologies. The becoming of the web has been characterized by this struggle. The outcome of the struggle, at present, is unclear. Surely the ideology of a free and natural market turned out to be a blunder. The idea that the market works as a pure environment of equal confrontation for ideas, projects, the productive quality and the utility of services has been wiped out by the sour truth of a war that monopolies have waged against the multitude of self-employed cognitive workers and against the slightly pathetic mass of micro-traders.

The struggle for survival was not won by the best and most successful, but by the one who drew his gun – the gun of violence, robbery, systematic theft, of the violation of all legal and ethical norms. The Bush-Gates alliance sanctioned the liquidation of the market, and at that point the phase of the internal struggle of the virtual class ended. One part of the virtual class entered the techno-military complex; another part (the large majority) was expelled from the enterprise and pushed to the margins of explicit proletarianization. On the cultural plane, the conditions for the formation of a social consciousness of the cognitariat are emerging, and this could be the most important phenomenon of the years to come, the only key to offer solutions to the disaster.

Dotcoms were the training laboratory for a productive model and for a market. In the end the market was conquered and suffocated by the corporations, and the army of self-employed entrepreneurs and venture micro-capitalists was robbed and dissolved. Thus a new phase began: the groups that became predominant in the cycle of the net-economy forge an alliance with the dominant group of the old economy (the Bush clan, representative of the oil and military industry), and this phase signals a blocking of the project of globalization. Neoliberalism produced its own negation, and those who were its most enthusiastic supporters become its marginalized victims.

With the dotcom crash, cognitive labor has separated itself from capital. Digital artisans, who felt like entrepreneurs of their own labor during the 1990s, are slowly realizing that they have been deceived, expropriated, and this will create the conditions for a new consciousness of cognitive workers. The latter will realize that despite having all the productive power, they have been expropriated of its fruits by a minority of ignorant speculators who are only good at handling the legal and financial aspects of the productive process. The unproductive section of the virtual class, the lawyers and the accountants, appropriate the cognitive surplus value of physicists and engineers, of chemists, writers and media operators. But they can detach themselves from the juridical and financial castle of semiocapitalism, and build a direct relation with society, with the users. Maybe then the process of the autonomous self-organization of cognitive labor will begin. This process is already under way, as the experiences of media activism and the creation of networks of solidarity from migrant labor show.

We needed to go through the dotcom purgatory, through the illusion of a fusion between labor and capitalist enterprise, and then through the hell of recession and endless war, in order to see the problem emerge in clear terms. On the one hand lies the useless and obsessive system of financial accumulation and privatization of public knowledge, the heritage of the old industrial economy. On the other hand, productive labor is being increasingly inscribed in the cognitive functions of society: cognitive labor is starting to see itself as a cognitariat, building institutions of knowledge, of creation, of care, of invention and of education that are autonomous from capital.

Fractal time and social pathology

In the net economy flexibility has evolved into a form of the fractalization of labor. Fractalization means the fragmentation of time-activity. The worker does not exist any more as a person. He is just the interchangeable producer of microfragments of recombinant semiosis which enters into the continuous flux of the network. Capital is no longer paying for the availability of the worker to be exploited for a long period of time; no longer paying a salary covering the entire range of economic needs of a working person. The worker (a mere machine possessing a brain that can be used for a fragment of time) is paid for his punctual performance. The working time is made fractal and cellular. Cells of time are on sale on the net, and the corporation can buy as many as it needs. The cellular phone is the tool that best defines the relationship between the fractal worker and recombinant capital.

Cognitive labor is an ocean of microscopic fragments of time that can be fragmented and recombined. The cellular phone can be seen as the assembly line of cognitive labor. What used to be the autonomy and the political power of the workforce has become the total dependence of cognitive labor on the capitalist organization of the global network, because time has been fragmented and made flexible in a fractal recombinant way. Where there used to be a refusal of work we find today a total dependence of emotions and thought on the flow of information. And the effect of this is a sort of nervous breakdown that strikes the global mind and provoked what we have called the dotcom-crash.

The dotcom-crash and the crisis of financial mass-capitalism can be viewed as an effect of the collapse of the economic investment of social desire. I use the word collapse in a sense that is not metaphorical, but rather a clinical description of what is going on in the western mind. I use the word collapse in order to express a real pathological crash of the psycho-social organism. What we have seen in the period following the first signs of economic crash, in the first months of the new century, is a psychopathological phenomenon, the collapse of the global mind. I see the present economic depression as the side effect of a psychic depression. The intense and prolonged investment of desire and of mental and libidinal energies in labor has created the psychic environment for the collapse which is now manifesting itself in the field of economic recession, in the field of military aggression and of a suicidal tendency.

The attention economy has become an important subject during the first years of the new century. Virtual workers have less and less time for attention, they are involved in a growing number of intellectual tasks, and they have no more time to devote to their own life, to love, tenderness, and affection. They take Viagra because they have no time for sexual preliminaries. Cellular communication has made possible a total occupation of the lifetime of workers. Its effect is the nervous pathology of the social relationship. The symptoms of it are quite evident: millions of boxes of Prozac sold every month, the epidemic of attention deficit disorders among youngsters, the diffusion of drugs like Ritalin to school children, and the spreading epidemic of panic.

The scenario of the first years of the new millennium seems to be dominated by a veritable wave of psychopathic behavior. The suicidal phenomenon is spreading well beyond the borders of Islamic fanatic martyrdom. Since the World Trade Center bombings, suicide has become the crucial political act on the global political scene.

Aggressive suicide should not be seen as a mere phenomenon of despair and aggression, but has to be seen as the declaration of the end. The suicidal wave seems to suggest that humankind has run out of time, and despair has became the prevalent way of thinking about the future.

So what? I have no answer. All we can do is what we are actually doing already: the self-organization of cognitive work is the only way to go beyond the psychopathic present. I don't believe that the world can be governed by reason. The utopia of Enlightenment has failed. But I think that the dissemination of self-organized knowledge can create a social framework containing infinite autonomous and self-reliant worlds.

The process of creating the network is so complex that it cannot be governed by human reason. The global mind is too complex to be known and mastered by subsegmental localized minds. We cannot know, we cannot control, we cannot govern the entire force of the global mind. But we can master the singular process of producing a singular world of sociality. This is autonomy today.

5. Frail psycho-sphere

Elephant

Michael Moore has dedicated a passionate documentary to the Columbine shooting (*Bowling for Columbine*, 2002), where he relates what anybody can see, the sale of firearms and the aggressiveness that feeds fear. But in his film *Elephant* (2003), Gus Van Sant interrogates the same episode from a deeper, more impalpable and hence more uncanny point of view. What has happened and what is happening in the mind of that generation coming of age at the turn of the millennium? What does it mean and where can its psychic fragility take us, endowed as it is with a terrifying technological and destructive power? Technological hyper-power and psychic fragility are the mix which defines the first video-electronic generation, especially its North American variant.

The disciplines of the natural sciences and psychiatry underestimate the effects of the psycho-cognitive mutation that traverse the first video-electronic generation. Politics ignores them or completely removes them, but if we want to understand something about what is happening in the society of the new millennium, we need to move our point of observation in this direction, towards the psycho-sphere. It is within the psycho-sphere that the effects of twenty years of info-invasion, nervous overload, mass psychopharmacology, sedatives, stimulants and euphoric sub-stances, of fractalization of working and existential time, of social inse-curity which translates into fear, solitude and terror, manifest themselves. Time-based psycho-bombs are exploding in the interconnected global mind. The effect is unpredictable.

In recent decades, the organism has been exposed to an increasing mass of neuro-mobilizing stimuli. The acceleration and intensification of nervous stimulants on the conscious organism seems to have thinned the cognitive film that we might call sensibility. The conscious organism needs to accelerate its cognitive, gestural, kinetic reactivity. The time available for responding to nervous stimuli has been dramatically reduced. This is perhaps why we seem to be seeing a reduction of the capacity for empathy. Symbolic exchange among human beings is elaborated without empathy, because it becomes increasingly difficult to perceive the existence of the body of the other in time. In order to experience the other as a sensorial body, you need time, time to caress and smell. The time for empathy is lacking, because stimulation has become too intense.

How did this happen? What is the cause of these disturbances of empathy whose signals are so evident in daily life, and in the events amplified by the media? Can we hypothesize a direct relationship between the expansion of the info-sphere (acceleration of stimuli and nervous solicitation, of the rhythms of cognitive response) and the crumbling of the sensory film that allows human beings to understand that which cannot be verbalized, that which cannot be reduced to codified signs?

Reducers of complexity such as money, information, stereotypes or digital network interfaces have simplified the relationship with the other, but when the other appears in flesh and blood, we cannot tolerate its presence, because it hurts our (in)sensibility. The video-electronic generation does not tolerate armpit or pubic hair. One needs perfect compatibility in order to interface corporeal surfaces in connection. Smooth generation. Conjunction finds its ways through hairs and the imperfections of exchange. It is capable of analogical reading, and heterogeneous bodies can understand each other even if they do not have an interfacing language.

The destruction of the interhuman sensory film has something to do with the techno-informational universe, but also with the capitalistic disciplining of corporeality. In the final phase of capitalist modernization, the emancipation of woman and her insertion into production has provoked an effect of rarefaction in the corporeal and intellectual contact with the child. The mother has disappeared or has reduced her presence in the experiential sphere of the first video-electronic generation. The combined effect of the so-called emancipation of women (which in reality has been the subjection of women to the circuit of capitalist production), and the diffusion of the televisual socializer has something to do with the contemporary psycho-political catastrophe.

Another upheaval is being prepared in the next generation. In many places, a process is taking place that could have significant consequences in the future. Millions of women in poor countries are forced to abandon their children in order to move to the West to look after the children of other mothers who cannot look after them because they are too busy with work. What phantasms of frustration and violence will grow in the minds of abandoned children? A people of hyper-armed children has invaded the world scene. It is doomed to get badly hurt, as in Vietnam. But unfortunately it hurts us too. We saw this in the pictures snapped at Abu Ghraib and other prisons of American infamy.

It is with glacial tenderness that Gus Van Sant shows us the neurotic mumbling, the anorexic hysterias and the relational incompetence of the Columbine generation (I am thinking about the splendidly bestial dialogue between the three girls in the canteen, when they decide to go shopping after having horrifically discussed friendship and its duties and the percentage of time that one should set aside for the dearest friends, in a minute quantification of affectivity). He shows us shining waiting rooms, luminous corridors traversed by psychos. Bodies that have lost contact with their soul and hence no longer know anything about their corporeality. Then everything happens while the sky rapidly moves by, as always in Gus Van Sant's films. In the suspended light of an ordinary day come the suicidal homicides. Everything happens within a few dilated minutes, recorded by closed circuit TV cameras: teenagers hide under tables, trying to avoid the bullets. There is no tragedy, no outcry; the ambulances are not yet there. The huge sky changes color. Dry, sparse shots. Not the terrifying crowds that we saw around Wall Street while the towers crashed. A quiet, peripheral massacre – reproducible, replicable, contagious.

Connective mutation

Elephant speaks of a generation that is emotionally disturbed and incapable of connecting thought and action. It speaks of a cognitive mutation that is unfolding in the context of a communicative transformation: the passage from conjunction to connection. The forms of conjunction are infinite, and connection is one of these. But within the concept of connecting there is an implicit specification: *connexio* implies the functionality of the materials being connected, a functional modeling that predisposes them to interfacing. While conjunction is a becoming other, in connection every element remains distinct, even though functionally interactive.

Conjunction is the encounter and fusion of rounded irregular forms that infiltrate in an imprecise, unrepeatable, imperfect, continuous way. Connection is the punctual and repeatable interaction of algorithmic functions, of straight lines and points that can be perfectly superimposed onto each other, inserting and detaching themselves according to discrete modalities of interaction. Modalities that establish a compatibility between diverse parts according to predetermined standards. The digitalization of communicative processes produces a sort of desensitization to the curve, to continuous processes of slow becoming, and a corresponding sensitization to code, sudden changes of state and the succession of discrete signs.

The first video-electronic generation is experiencing a mutation, and the social, political and technical future depends on the effects of this mutation. But in the tradition of the cognitive sciences, the notion of mutation is not acceptable, because the epistemological foundations of these sciences remain anchored to a premise of a structuralist nature. In effect, cognitivism considers the human mind as a device that functions according to innate and unchangeable rules. Cognitivism cannot see how the environment acts on the concrete and particular modes of functioning of the mind. For this reason, the notion of a dynamic interaction between mental activity and the environment in which minds enter into communication is inadmissible. For the cognitive sciences, the technical complexity of communication is incapable of modifying the modalities of cognition, even if certain cognitivists depart from this founding principle. In *Cognition and Reality*, for example, Ulric Neisser speaks of a cognitive ecology and recognizes the possibility of a dynamic interaction between the environment in which the mind develops and its modes of functioning (1976).

Acceleration, language, identity

The acceleration of the circulation of information, the mass of information that we receive, decode, digest, and must respond to in order to maintain the rhythm of economic, affective and existential exchanges, brings with it a crisis of the faculty of verbalization that manifests itself in various forms: autism and the dizzying escalation of dyslexia in the youngest generations, particularly in the social and professional classes most involved in the new technologies of communication.

Digitalization seems to open up a double movement of reformatting. Verbal language is being replaced by forms of communication that are more rapid, more synthetic and more agile in carrying out different tasks simultaneously, according to the multitask method. But the acceleration of impulses provokes stress in the physical organism and demands a psychotropic reformatting of perception and cognitive interaction, through the use of psychopharmacological drugs or the pure and simple deactivation of empathy (which slows down cognitive rhythm) and the attenuation of certain sensory levels such as smell and touching, already reshaped by the acceleration of writing.

In general we can say that the expansion of a specific cognitive function redefines the whole of cognition. The exposure of the conscious organism to video-electronics amplifies competencies of a configurational type such as the ability to decode complex visual ensembles or to develop multiple processes of interaction simultaneously. But at the same time it reshapes other competencies, such as the ability to react emotionally to stimuli that are drawn out in time or the capacity to perceive temporal depth.

The modalities of memorization depend on the mind's capacity to store information that has left a deep impression, was active over a long period of time or in repetitive fashion. Memorization modifies the conscious organism and shapes its identity, given that identity can be defined as a dynamic accumulation of the memory of places and relations forming the continuity of an experience.

But what happens to memory when the flow of information explodes, expands enormously, besieges perception, occupies the whole of available mental time, accelerates and reduces the mind's time of exposure to the single informational impression? What happens here is that the memory of the past thins out and the mass of present information tends to occupy the whole space of attention. The greater the density of the info-sphere, the scarcer is the time available for memorization. The briefer the mind's lapse of exposure to a single piece of information, the more tenuous will be the trace left by this information. In this way, mental activity tends to be compressed into the present, the depth of memory is reduced and thus the perception of the historical past and even of existential diachrony tends to disappear.

And if it's true that identity is in large part connected to what has dynamically settled in personal memory (places, faces, expectations, illusions), it is possible to hypothesize that we are moving towards a progressive disidentification, where organisms are increasingly recording a flow that unfolds in the present and leaves no deep imprint because of the rapidity with which it appears to the eye and settles in memory. The thickening of the info-spheric crust and the increase in quantity and intensity of the incoming informational material thus produces the effect of a reduction of the sphere of singular memory. The things that an individual remembers (images, etc.) work towards the construction of an impersonal memory, homogenized, uniformly assimilated and thinly elaborated because the time of exposure is so fast it doesn't allow for a deep personalization.

Cybertime, eroticism, desensitization

It seems to me that the fundamental question of the current mutation – the mutation that flows through individual organisms, populations and the entire planet – can be found at the intersection of electronic and organic cyberspace. Young people are naturally the most exposed to the effects of this mutation, because the invasive power of cyberspace has impacted on them to the full, and as a consequence their potential to adapt cybertemporally (that is the potential of their cognitive, psychic and psycho-physical apparatus) is subject to an extreme solicitation. The essential problem is that the rhythms of the technological mutation are a lot faster than those of the mental mutation. Hence the expansion of cyberspace is incommensurably faster than the human brain's capacity to expand and adapt (cybertime). We can increase the length of time an organism is exposed to information, but experience can't be intensified beyond a certain limit. Acceleration provokes an impoverishment of experience, given that we are exposed to a growing mass of stimuli that we can't digest in the intensive modes of enjoyment and knowledge. Spheres of relationality and behavior that require an extended period of attention such as those of affectivity, eroticism and deep comprehension, are disturbed, subject to a contraction. In these conditions of acceleration and information overload, automatism tends to become the prevalent form of reaction to stimuli, in the sense that automatic reactions are those that don't demand reflection or a conscious and emotional reaction. They are standard reactions, implicit in the preformatted chain of actions and reactions of the homogenized info-sphere.

The digitalization of the communicative environment and even of the perceptive environment without a doubt acts on the sensibility of human organisms. But how do we address this problematic? What instruments of analysis, what criteria of evaluation allow us to speak of sensibility, of taste, of enjoyment and suffering, eroticism and sensuality? We have no other instrument but ourselves, our antennae, our bodies, our psychic

and erotic reactivity. Moreover, the filter of the observer can have a dis-
torting effect. And yet the feeling of rarefaction of contact, coldness and
contraction are at the core of our contemporary pathologies, particularly
evident in the younger generation. The sphere of eroticism is particularly
prone to them.

After the end of the avant-gardes and their infiltration into the circuit
of social communication, aesthetic stimulation in the form of advertising,
television, design, packaging, web design etc., is increasingly widespread,
pervasive, insistent, indissociable from the informational stimulation to
which it has become complementary. The conscious-feeling organism is
enveloped in a flux of signs that are not simply the bearers of information,
but also factors of perceptive stimulation and excitation. In the past, artistic experience was founded on the sensorial centrality of catharsis. The
work of art created a wave of involvement and excitement that rushed
forward towards a climax, a cathartic state of agitation comparable to
orgasmic release. In its classical, as well as romantic and modern con-
ceptions, beauty was identifiable with the moment of completion, an
overcoming of the tension implicit in the relationship between the feeling
organism and the world: catharsis, harmony, sublime detachment. Reaching harmony is an event that can be compared to orgasmic release following the excitement of contact between bodies. Muscle tension relaxes
in the fullness of pleasure. In the happy perception of one's own body
and the surrounding environment what is at play is an essential question
of rhythm, time and lived temporalities. But if, into the circle of excitement, we introduce an inorganic element such as electronics and impose
an acceleration of stimuli and a contraction of psychophysical reaction
times, something ends up changing in the organism and its forms of erotic
reaction. Orgasm is replaced by a series of excitations without release.
Orgasm is no longer the prelude to any accomplishment. Inconclusive
excitation takes the place of orgasmic release. This is something like the
feeling that is conveyed to us by digital art, the coldness of video art, the
inconclusive cyclical nature of the work of Tinguely or the music of Philip
Glass. Not only aesthetics but also eroticism seems to be implicated in
this inorganic acceleration of the relationship between bodies. The video
installation, *The Wind* (2002), by Eija Liisa Ahtila, consisting of three
screens on which scenes of destruction, attempts at contact with the body
of the other and devastating crises of solitude unfold, is the most direct
inquiry I know of into a form of psychopathology that, at the beginning
of the new millennium, is tending to become epidemic.

Traveling the circuits of social communication, the erotic object is multiplied to the point of becoming omnipresent. But excitation is no longer the prelude to any conclusion and multiplies desire to the point of shattering it. The unlimited nature of cyberspace endows experience with a kind of inconclusiveness. Aggressiveness and exhaustion follow from this unlimited opening of the circuits of excitation. Isn't this perhaps an explanation of the erotic anxiety that leads to de-eroticization and that mix of hypersexuality and asexuality that characterizes post-urban life? The city was the place where the human body encountered the human body, the site of the gaze, contact, slow emotion and pleasure. In the post-urban dimension of the cyberspatial sprawl, contact seems to become impossible, replaced by precipitous forms of experience that overlap with commercialization and violence. Slow emotion is rare and improbable. And the very slowness of emotion is transformed little by little into a commodity, an artificial condition that can be exchanged for money. Time is scarce – time can be exchanged for money. Time, an indispensable dimension of pleasure, is cut into fragments that can no longer be enjoyed. Excitation without release replaces pleasure.

In the cultural phenomenology of late modernity, the mutation we are speaking of can be connected to the transition period that takes places from the 1960s and 1970s to the 1980s and 1990s. The years of hippy culture were centered around a project of eroticization of the social, of universal contact between bodies. In the transition period that coincides with the introduction of electronic communications technologies into the social circuit, the punk phenomenon explodes. Punk cries out desperately against the rarefaction of contact, against the post-urban desert, and reacts with a kind of hysterical self-destructiveness. The transition towards the postmodern and hyper-technological dimension was regis-tered by the New Wave of the early 1980s, which in its most extreme form defined itself as No Wave. No Wave doesn't mean immobility or constant flow without undulation; on the contrary, it means infinite frag-mentation of the wave, it means nano-wave, infinitesimal agitation of the musculature, subliminal, uncontrollable micro-excitation: nervous break-down. Between the 1970s and 1980s, the irruption of heroin into the existential experience of the post-urban transition was a part of this process of adaptation to a condition of excitation without release. Heroin allows for a switching-off, a disconnection from the circuit of uninter-rupted overexcitement, a kind of attenuation of tension. The collective organism of western society looked for a slowing down in the massive consumption of heroin, or else, in a complementary fashion, looked to cocaine as a way of keeping up with the pace. What was taking place here was the shift in info-spheric speed that made it possible to subjugate human time to the regime of absolute and uninterrupted exploitation of the neuro-telematic network – the flexibilization of work.

The obsession with identity

The crisis of the internationalist perspective after 1989 marks the outbreak of a civil war over the question of identity *on a planetary scale*. This is the prospect that has unfolded over the course of the 1990s. Metropolitan cosmopolitanism remains limited to the virtual class, to the globalized stratum of the planetary network. The great majority of humanity remains excluded from the cabled circuit of hypermodern cosmopolitanism, and is gripped by its obsessions with identity. Residual localisms acquire a desperate energy but this signals the beginning of the crisis of modern universalism.

What does universalism mean? We can talk of universalism when confronted with a perspective of ethical, political and existential value that possesses a universal normative force beyond cultural differences. Materialist dialectics opposed bourgeois universalism with proletarian particularism, the negative force of a partisan interest that contained within itself the nucleus of a higher, more fully human form of social relation. But this particularism still possessed (dialectically) a universalist horizon. Affirming sectarian working class particularity meant, in the dialectical vision, posing the conditions for a higher universality. This ideological schema is clearly of Hegelian, historicist derivation. But this does not take away the fact that internationalism was something more concrete than a moral proposition.

Internationalism was not an abstract value to pursue, but a fact of collective experience that lived in the struggle of workers against capitalism, and in the unity of proletarian interests that knew no borders. Workers have the same interests in every place across the globe: to appropriate growing quotients of the wealth that they themselves have produced, and to reduce the time of their dependence upon wage labor. The stronger workers are in one point of the cycle, the stronger workers are in all other points of the cycle. This elementary truth did not allow us to foresee the profound cultural change which followed the capitalist attack of the 1980s.

The reemergence on the world scene of peoples is the sign of working class defeat: peoples are the particularity that cannot be rendered dialectical, the particularity without a universal project, the idiot particularity.

In the years when the movements were at their height, fascism, in all its forms, appeared to us as an epoch that was dead and gone forever; or, at most, it appeared as a brutal instrument of repression. We thought a new type of totalitarianism was possible, but under the banners of social democracy, of a concentrated and technological hyper-development. Only social democracy, it seemed to us, was capable of dividing the movement of workers and subordinating it to reformism and statism. The scenario since 1990s has been completely different. It is no longer true that the decisive forces are capital and the working class. As in a game of mirrors, the context has been fragmented, multiplied, overturned. Capital and working class continue to confront each other, but in a manner that overturns the relation they had in the 1960s: the initiative (which then belonged to the workers) has today decisively shifted to international finance capital. At the same time, two other figures have appeared: the virtual class, that is the cycle of globalized mental labor; and the residual class, the shapeless mass of populations excluded from (or who were never part of) the production cycle, who aggressively press to conquer a space of survival and recognition in the planetary spectacle.

The word revolution no longer means anything within this new configuration but then neither does the phrase political democracy. A political level common to the figures of globalized fragmentary labor no longer exists, because they lack a shared social foundation. While capital courses through them all (because it continues to be the agent of a generalized codification), the figures of mental labor are simultaneously fragmentary in their innermost constitution, and global in their extrinsic relation, mediated by technology.

Fascism and identification

Fascism is a shapeless word. For a long time I strove to find a concept able to define the different (and contradictory) forms of authoritarianism, of nationalistic or ethnic aggression and so on, but without success. In his article "Il fascismo eterno," Umberto Eco recognizes that "the characteristics cannot be marshaled into a system, many are mutually contradictory and are typical of other forms of despotism and fanaticism. But it is sufficient for one to be present for a fascist nebula to coagulate."

There follows a list of Ur-fascism's characteristics: the cult of tradition, the refusal of modernism, action for action's sake, the fear of difference, and so on. But, as interesting and pertinent as these characteristics are, Eco himself recognizes that the effort of definition seems ultimately to end in frustration because its object continues to escape. For example, after having said that fascism is contrary to modernism, it must be recognized that historic fascism played a role in the modernization of society in both Italy and Germany. In the absence, then, of a satisfactory and comprehensive definition, we run the risk of defining fascism as everything that disgusts us, and of identifying fascism, simply, as the party of imbecility and violence: as the party of evil. And this, naturally, doesn't work, it doesn't define anything. The problem is that to which we are referring by using this word fascism which is imprecise and historically far too dated, is an extremely vast field of forms of life, behaviors, ideologies and prejudices that have, in the last analysis, a single element in common: the obsession with definition. The obsession to define is, in the last analysis, the characteristic common to the field of phenomena that we define as fascism. This is why this object is so difficult to define.

Fascism, in its maximum conceptual extension (encompassing nationalism and religious fundamentalism, political authoritarianism, sexual aggression and so on) can be brought back to a fundamental obsession: the obsession with identity, the obsession with belonging, with origin, with recognizability. This obsession has grown, extended itself, exploded over the course of our century, precisely because our century is a century of deterritorialization, of cultural contamination and de-identification. The pressure that seems to fundamentally guide those behaviors which fall within the ambit of fascism is the pressure to recognize ourselves as identical, identifiable, and therefore belonging to a community (of language, faith, race) based upon origin. Only origin bears witness to belonging, and as we know, origin is an illusion, a legend, an attribute that is more or less shared, but unfounded. Ethnic identity does not exist any more than linguistic identity. While each of us comes from a history of crossbreeding and contaminations that can neither be attested nor authenticated, there are illusions of ethnic belonging; while each of us speaks our own dialect that can never be fundamentally translatable by another speaker, there are illusions of linguistic comprehension. Living together is premised on these. The more the field of ethnic identifiability, of comprehensibility, of origin, are perturbed, the more acute becomes the need to identify, to the point of obsession.\

Totalitarian code

In the end, the inhuman appears as the dominant form of human relations: reaction devolved to a development of capital that, even as it proceeds triumphantly, excludes and crystallizes growing sections of the planetary nervous system, and secretes inhumanity. After having subordinated the working class variable, capital readies itself for its new, titanic enterprise: subordinating the entire cycle of human cognitive activity into an automated system that is cabled on a number of levels: the economic, technological, psychochemical – and perhaps in the future, also the biogenetic. But the residues that this enterprise leaves along its course are immense, corresponding to the majority of the human population.

After having incorporated working class autonomy in technique, and after having eliminated every alternative perspective, capital imposes itself as the accumulation of automatic processes that are no longer governable or opposable. Techno-social interfaces progressively connect towards the transformation of the global economy into a hive mind that functions according to prescribed goals and is cabled in the techno-linguistic garb of its human terminals. At this point, the biocomputer superorganism reads the human and discards it as noise. This process leads to the creation of a super-identity completely indifferent to identities of origin (of sex, race, faith, nationality). But in the process of this superidentity's formation, an enormous quantity of human material is discarded: the majority of humanity, which remains outside the cabled circuit of the globalized techno-economy. This material residue identifies itself through aggressive cults, founded on the illusion of an originary authenticity in need of restoration. Only the affirmation of an identity makes survival possible in a world increasingly dense with conflicting territorial projects, in a world dominated by the paradox of growing wealth that produces an expanding misery.

In the horizon of evolution, the problem of collective happiness and liberation comes to be posed in terms that are completely asymmetrical to those we have known in the past. How will the human singularity reproduce itself in the sphere of the posthuman? Harmony, happiness, awareness: how can these be singularized in the sphere of the cabled global mind? The universality to which dialectical thought aspired was the result of the very process of particularities' capacity to constitute themselves as a conscious subject, and therefore to surpass the particular. Instead we are now dealing with a different idea of universality: the abstract universality of code that semiotizes every fragment of the existing without respecting any pulsation of living human particularity.

The century is ending under the sign of an inhuman universality, the universality of code, of abstraction that manifests in money, in the circulation of information and finances. Therefore an abstract and disincarnated totalitarianism takes the place of the machine of universal semiotization. Facing it is the massive return of the residual human, of the body, of blood and soil, of tradition and identity: the rancorous and aggressive reaffirmation of particularity against every other particularity, in the name of no universality.

Ethics, sensitivity, sensibility

An old American officer, in charge of training Marines going to wage war somewhere, recounted in *Newsweek* something interesting about his own experience: "I used to do this job in the 70s, during the war in Vietnam. In those years it took six months to train a young person to be prepared to kill a human being. Now I am doing the same job in Iraq, but things have changed. The young men come here already trained. They come here ready to kill."

What has befallen the first post-alphabetic generation, those whom have learned more words from a machine than from their mothers (those whom some call the post-human generation)?

Should it be treated as an ethical question? In my view, ethics come out of sensibility. I don't see an alternative efficacious ethical discourse that does not found itself on self-love. And self-love cannot but be love of the other. Self-contempt and cynicism go together. And at the heart of the ethical question is the problem of sensibility (or maybe of sensitivity?).

In Italian 'sensibilità' and 'sensitività' have a different meaning to 'sensibility' and 'sensitivity' in English.

Sensibility is the capacity to grasp the meaning of that which cannot be expressed in words. Sensitivity is the capacity to feel the skin of the other as pleasure. But when, between the two faculties, one determines a deviation, the distrubance of the epidermic perception of the other becomes the incapacity to understand the meaning of signs that eminate from the other.

The tendential fall of the knowledge of pleasure

On June 19th, 2007 *Le Monde* reported that Durex, the prophylactic giant, the grand corporate producers of condoms, had commissioned an investigation by the Harris Interactive Institute.

Twenty countries of different cultures were selected. In each country

1,000 people were asked a simple question: how satisfied they were with sex. Only 44% of the interviewees responded that they were happy with their sex lives.

Maybe it can be said that post-modern bipeds experience sophisticated pleasures in labor and war; who knows? But certainly love doesn't enjoy great success with the public, so much so that it is hard to believe that 44% told their intimate truth, the one that reflects their deepest feelings, whereas we can be certain that the remainder are really unhappy.

The explanations that sexologists, psychologists and sociologists offer on these matters are in general of little interest: the liberation of sexual customs, the crisis of desire, the commodification of the human body, the becoming banal of sex through media. These are explanations that offer little. Lucy Vincent, a neurobiologist interviewed in June 2007 in *Le Parisien*, offered an intelligent, if slightly forced, interpretation: "it is not accorded much attention." We are no longer capable of according attention to ourselves and those that live around us. Drawn into the spiral of competition we are no longer capable of understanding anything about the other.

Attention, the cognitive faculty that makes possible the full perception of a mental object (our own body, for example, or the body of a person that we caress) is available in limited quantities, so much so that in recent years some economists (the real gravediggers of the human soul) have begun to speak of the attention economy, and when a resource becomes the object of necrophiliac science, it is to say that it has become a scarce resource.

Attention is a scarce resource, so it is understandable that there are techniques to optimize it.

The obsession with the (vanishing) body

The precarious generation grew up when the internet was becoming a prosthesis of social language. They have been exposed to a continuous flow of electronic stimuli, altering the modes of linguistic learning, the rhythms of attention, and memory and imagination.

McLuhan wrote that during the passage from the alphabetic to the electronic sphere, mythological thought tends to take the place of the logical-critical thought. But what about the affective and psychic sphere of the video-electronic generation?

We know that in the Western world millions of children are every day taking Ritalin in order to treat the symptoms of the so-called attention deficit disorders. Focusing on an object for a certain deal of time is becoming an impossible task for a large number of kids: attention tends to change immediately its focus, looking for a new object. There is a direct a relationship between the exposure time of the mind to the video-electronic stimulus and the growing volatility of attention. Never in the history of humankind has the mind of a child been exposed to such a fast and invading bombardment of info impulses. It is obvious that this acceleration is producing unpredictable effects on the cognitive domain.

Language learning has much to do with the bodily relationship. Language and socialization have always been mediated by affectivity, by the reassuring and pleasant contact with the mother's body. During the last decades the body of the mother has been separated from the child's body. In neoliberal society women are forced to work away from home, and so they are distanced from their babies, in conditions of psycho-physical stress, anxiety and affective impoverishment.

Info-machines have taken the place of the mother, changing the process of language learning. Certainly the first video-electronic generation did enjoy the mother's bodily presence much less than in the past times. The bodily and affective contact was a factor of singularization of language, and it is lost. Emotion and word tend to divert in these conditions. Desire becomes a dimension which is more and more separated from verbalization, from conscious processing of information. Emotions without words tend to feed psychopathology and violence. Acting without verbal communication is closed to aggression. Words without emotion feed a sociality which is poorer and poorer, reduced to the logic of giving and receiving.

The verbal processing of information and of emotion that is connected to information is compressed in ever accelerated times, and is giving way to a disturbance of emotionality and verbalization. Aphasia can be interpreted as a consequence of the growing distance between info-stimulation and the time needed for the elaboration of info-stimuli. We may see an effect of this acceleration also in the phenomenon of dyslexia? that is especially affecting cognitive workers, those who are exposed to the rhythm of electronic communication. To read a text from the beginning to the end seems to be an impossible task for managers.

Desire dwells in conjunction, and is killed by connection. Connection means a relationship between formatted segments; making desingularized bodies compatible. Conjunction means singular, unrepeatable communication between round bodies. Connection means integration of smooth bodies in a space which is no space and in a time which is no time.

The process of change underway in our time is centered on the shift from conjunction to connection as the paradigm of exchange between conscious organisms. The leading factor of this change is the insertion of the electronic in the organic, the proliferation of artificial devices in the organic universe, the body, communication and society. But the effect of this change is a transformation of the relationship between consciousness and sensibility, and increasing desensitization in the exchange of signs.

Conjunction is the meeting and fusion of round and irregular shapes that are continuously weaseling their way about with no precision, repetition or perfection. Connection is the punctual and repeatable interaction of algorithmic functions, straight lines and points that overlap perfectly, and plug in or out according to discrete modes of interaction that render the different parts compatible to a pre-established standard. The shift from conjunction to connection as the predominant mode of interaction of conscious organisms is a consequence of the gradual digitalization of signs and the increasing mediatization of relations.

The digitalization of communicative processes induces a sort of desensitization to the curve, the continuous process of slow becoming; and a sort of sensitization to the code, sudden changes of state and series of discrete signs.

Conjunction entails a semantic criterion of interpretation. When the other enters in conjunction with you, he is sending signs that you must interpret the meaning of, by tracing if necessary the intention, the context, the shade, the unsaid. On the contrary, connection requires a criterion of interpretation that is purely syntactic. The interpreter must recognize a sequence and be able to carry out the operation foreseen by the general syntax (or operating system); there can be no margins for ambiguity in the exchange of messages, nor can the intention be manifest though nuances. The gradual translation of semantic differences into syntactic differences is the process that led from modern scientific rationalism to cybernetics and eventually made the creation of a digital web possible.

Conjunction is a process of 'becoming other.' In contrast, in connection, each element remains distinct and interacts only functionally. Singularities change when they conjoin – they become something other than what they were before their conjunction. The combination of asignifying signs gives rise to the emergence of meaning which previously did not exist.

Rather than a fusion of segments, connection entails a simple effect of machine functionality. The functionality of the connecting materials is implicit in the connection as a functional modeling that prepares them for interfacing and inter-operability. In order for connection to be possible, segments must be linguistically compatible. Connection requires a prior process whereby the elements that need to connect are made compatible. Indeed the digital web extends through the progressive reduction of an increasing number of elements to a format, a standard and a code that makes compatible different elements.

Connected bodies are subjected to a kind of progressive inability to feel pleasure, and forced to choose the way of simulating pleasure: the shift from touch to vision, from hairy bodies to smooth connectable bodies. The control on the body does not come from outside. The control is built inside, in the very relationship between self-perception and identity.

When the info-sphere becomes hyper-speedy, hyper-thick, and the impulses are proliferating beyond any limit, we become less and less able to elaborate in a conscious way on the emotional impulses reaching our skin, our sensitivity, our brain. Consciousness is detached from sensitivity, and subjugated by the connective machine.

Autistic behavior can be described as the effect of the inability to feel the other's emotionality, and to project in the other's body pleasure and pain that we feel in our body. Lack of empathy seems to be an endemic effect of the growing time of the exposure of the mind to the accelerated virtual info-sphere.

The acceleration and intensification of nervous stimulants on the conscious organism seem to have thinned the cognitive film that we might call sensibility.

Pornography grabs the attention quickly, you don't need to work for it, you don't need to feel empathy, you just watch. Almost like an autistic state of mind. It's not necessary to try and understand the feelings of the other person, it's not about them, they are objects or tools in the need for satisfaction. The bodies are deprived of everything that makes them human by the lurker.

In this condition of autistic excitation without fulfillment social behavior tends to become something similar to obsessive rituals. In the year 1907, Freud wrote an essay on the symptomatology of obsession and the religious rituals. The ritual, he says, has something to do with the obsession, because it has the same character of irrealization and of compulsive repetition. Irrealization and compulsive repetition are peculiar in religious behavior as in pornographic sex. Religious behavior, like pornographic sexuality, performs a ritual which, in its nature, has the stigma of the obsessive neurosis: repetition of acts that are devoid of semantic meaning and devoid of special efficiency.

Obsession: compulsive repetition of a ritual which does not fulfill its aim. The real scope of the ritual is the conjuration which holds the (rite maker's) own world together. Porn in general has something to do with the ritual.

It seems that in the experience of the first connective generation the bodily relationship is becoming growingly difficult, embarrassing. So the ritual is taking the place of pleasure, and porn becomes the repetition of an act of seeing which does not attain its emotional end.

I'm not reclaiming any authenticity for the erotic self; I'm not fantasizing about the golden age of sexual happiness. I'm just interested in finding the signs of a pathology in the current proliferation of pornography: namely a pathology of emotionality. This pathology, which is latent in every kind of pornographic product, is highlighted by the mediatization, and especially by the net proliferation of porn. Since image and emotion are separated, the pornographic act (of vision) does not produce the emotional effect we are expecting. So we repeat the act (of vision).

The net is the place of endless replication – therefore it is the ideal place of pornographic ritual. Stimulus hypertrophy is the general frame which generates current obsession in the saturated info-sphere.

During their long evolution, human beings have slowly learned to elaborate the stimulus of sexual excitation: the entire history of culture can be viewed as a way to elaboration of the sexual desire. Through imagination and language human beings manage to balance the stimulus coming from the environment, and the psychic and sexual response to it.

We're now living in the age of info-proliferation. The saturation of the info-sphere provokes a stimulus overload, and this has an obvious cognitive effect: time for attention decreases. But affective attention takes time, and cannot be shortened or fastened. This leads to a disorder in the emotional elaboration of meaning. Affective attention suffers a kind of contraction, and it is forced to find ways of adaptation: the organism adopts tools for simplification, and it tends to smooth out the living psychic response, to repackage affective behavior in a frozen and fastened framework.

The focal point is the shortening of time for emotional elaboration: pornography is in turn one of the causes of this saturation, and one of the effects, or, better, one of the symptoms of it. Pornography concurs to the saturation of the info-sphere, and it is simultaneously an escape from the disturbed psycho-sphere.

What is the meaning of the word emotion? Emotion is the meeting point between body and cognition: it is a bodily elaboration of information that is reaching our mind. The time of emotionality can be fast (very fast) and can be slow. But sexual emotion needs slow time for elaboration. The time of caresses cannot be shortened by automatic engines, although pharmacology can fasten the sexual reactions, and speed up erection. The use of sexual stimulants like Viagra has not so much to do with impotence, but with haste, and emotional disturbances.

The electronic excitation conveyed through the entire mediascape puts the sensitive organism in a state of permanent electrocution. Time for linguistic elaboration of a single input is reduced as the number of inputs increase, and the speed of the input gets higher. Sex is not speaking anymore. It is rather babbling, and faltering, and it is also suffering of it. Too few words, too little time to talk. Too little time to feel. Porn is an exercise in emotional automation and uniformity of the emotional time of response. Don't miss the implication between permanent electrocution, the shortening of linguistic attentive elaboration and atrophy of emotional response. Pornography is just the visible surface of this neuro short circuit.

The connective generation is showing signs of an epidemic of emotional atrophy. The disconnection between language and sexuality is striking. Pornography is the ultimate form of this disconnection.

When a group of very young men in a northern Italian place murdered a young girl after harassing her, the investigators who studied the case were stunned by the inability of the youngsters to verbalize their act, their feeling, and their motivation. Syntactic elaboration reduced to zero. Monosyllables. Onomatopoeic sounds.

Sensitivity is invested in this turn, and it enters a process of re-formatting; the new format is the smooth, the connectible. Sexual imagination is overwhelmed by the hairless smoothness of the digital image. The perception of the real body of the other in daily life is becoming obnoxious: hard to touch, hard to feel, hard to enjoy.

This pathological turn of the psycho-sphere seems to me the main feature of the current anthropological mutation which encompasses social change, and politics and the global tragedy of terror that is devastating the perception of the bodies that are surrounding and touching our own.

The obsessive repetition of a gesture that is no longer able to fulfill its aim, the hopeless effort to grasp a pleasure that we have no time to nurture, all this has very much to do with the coming back of violence, of war and of torture into the world scene.

Both in the western and in the Islamic world, we are undergoing a daily instigation to fear, to aggression, to hate. The bodily imagination is disturbed by the growing all-pervading ecology of fear. Although never erased from the hidden reality of history, for a long time torture has been rejected by the consciousness and excluded from the field of social visibility. After the defeat of Nazism, torture has been considered the ultimate mark of inhumanity.

But during the last few years, just in the dawn of the new century, torture has resurfaced, abruptly becoming a normal tool of political action. Torturers and their accomplices are officially sitting in power in the US, in Russia and in many other places. Torturers are showing their deeds to their friends by the means of videophonic display and the internet. Beheading is proudly shown as a demonstration of bravery and religious faith.

How could it happen? Why has social sensitivity turned to barbarism and inhumanity? We have to understand what is happening in the deepness of bodily perception, if we want to understand what is happening on the surface of terrorist and military action. Pornography and torture have little in common, if anything. But their media diffusion takes place in the same vacuum generated by the atrophy of emotionality. The inability to feel pleasure has its counterpart in the inability to perceive horror as horror.

6. Dark Desires

Discomfort and repression

Whether directly or indirectly, Sigmund Freud's notion of repression greatly influenced the anti-authoritarian thought of the twentieth century. He best explains it in *Civilization and its Discontents*[1]

> We cannot fail to be struck by the similarity between the process of civilization and the libidinal development of the individual. Other instincts are induced to displace the conditions for their satisfaction, to lead them into other paths. In most cases this process coincides with that of the sublimation (of instinctual aims)... It is impossible to overlook the extent to which civilization is built up upon a renunciation of instinct, how much it presupposes precisely the non-satisfaction (by suppression, repression or some other means?) of powerful instincts. This 'cultural frustration' dominates the large field of social relationships between human beings. As we already know, it is the cause of the hostility against which all civilizations have to struggle (1929: 34).

Freud regards repression as an unwavering and constitutive trait of social relations. During the twentieth century, between the 1930s and 1960s, European critical theory interrogated the relationship between the anthropological aspect of alienation and the historical character of liberation. On the one hand, in the *Critique of dialectical reason* (1964), Jean Paul Sartre recognized the anthropologically constitutive – and hence insuperable – character of alienation. On the other hand, the historicist and dialectical variant of Marxist theory regarded alienation as a historically determined phenomenon that could be overcome through the abolition of capitalist social relations. In his 1929 essay, whilst criticizing the naivety of dialectical thinking, Freud anticipated the main issues of the debate:

> The communists believe that they have found the path to deliverance from our evils. According to them, man is wholly good and well-disposed to his neighbor; but the institution of private property has corrupted his nature... If private property were abolished, all wealth held in common, and everyone allowed to share in the enjoyment of it, ill-will and hostility would disappear among men... I have no concern with any economic criticism of the communist system; I cannot enquire into whether the abolition of private property is expedient or advantageous. But I am able to recognize that the psychological premises on which the system is based are an untenable illusion (1929: 50).

I am not interested in reopening the debates between either historicism and existentialism or Marxism and psychoanalysis: these ought to be consigned to the historians of the philosophy of the twentieth century; what I want to point out is their shared philosophical framework and common analytical premise, reliant on the identification of modern civilization with a system based on repression.

According to Freud, like any other system of civilization, modern capitalism is founded on the necessary removal of the individual libido and on the sublimating organization of the collective libido. This same intuition is inflected in various ways throughout the thought of the twentieth century.

In Freudian psychoanalysis, this discontent is constitutive and insurmountable and the goal of psychoanalytical therapy is to cure, through language and anamnesis, the neuroses it produces in us. Existentialism-inspired philosophical culture shares Freud's belief in the insuperability of constitutive alienation and the repression of libidinal drives.

On the contrary, in Marxist and anti-authoritarian theory, repression is socially determined and can be removed by an act of society that frees the productive and desiring energies existing in its real movement.

Nonetheless, repression plays a crucial role in both philosophies because, as a concept, it serves as an explanation for the neurotic pathologies that psychological therapy takes as its object, as well as the capitalist social contradiction that revolutionary movements aim to abolish to create the conditions of possibility for the overcoming of exploitation and alienation itself.

During the 1960s and 1970s the concept of repression provided the backdrop to every political debate inspired by desire. The political value of desire was always pitted against dispositifs of repression, and these often revealed to be a conceptual and political trap. For instance, following the 1977 wave of arrests of the February and March insurrections, the Italian movement decided to gather around the issue of repression at the Bologna conference. This could have been a conceptual mistake: in choosing repression as the main issue under discussion, we entered the narrative machine of power and lost the ability to imagine forms of life that were asymmetrical to and thus independent from it.

Anyhow, by the end of the twentieth century the whole question of repression seemed to melt into thin air and disappear from the scene. Rather than neuroses produced by a repression of libido, the dominant pathologies of our times are schizoid and result from an eruption of expression: Just do it.

Structure and desire

The anti-authoritarianism of the 1970s operated within a Freudian conceptual framework, though expanding and subverting its historical outlook. In *Eros and Civilization* Herbert Marcuse proclaims the actuality of the liberation of collective eros. Repression constricts the potential of technology and knowledge and prevents their full development; yet critical subjectivity actually unfolds by enabling the full expression of the libidinal and productive potential of society, and creating the conditions for a full realization of the pleasure principle. The analysis of modern society intersects the description of the mechanisms of discipline that repressively shape social institutions and public discourse. The recent publication of Michel Foucault's 1979 lectures (2008) compels us to shift the barycenter of Foucault's thought away from repressive discipline and towards the creation of dispositifs of biopolitical control. However, Foucault still operates in his own way within the 'repressive' paradigm throughout his work on the genealogy of modernity (in particular, in *History of Madness*, *The Birth of the Clinic*, and *Discipline and Punish*).

Even Gilles Deleuze and Félix Guattari, despite the openly declared abandonment of the Freudian framework in *Anti-Oedipus*, operate within the field of problematization outlined by Freud in 1929: desire is the motor of the movement that traverses both society and the path of singularity, whilst desiring creativity has to constantly come to terms with the repressive war machines wedged by capitalism into every fold of existence and imagination. The concept of desire cannot be flattened out by a reading of it in terms of 'repression.' In *Anti-Oedipus* desire is opposed to lack. The philosophy of dialectics flourished and the politics of the twentieth century built its (mis)fortunes on the notion of lack: a notion of dependency rather than autonomy. Lack is a product, determined by the regime of economics, religion and psychiatric domination.

Rather than lack, it is desire as creation that gives ground to processes of erotic and political subjectivation. In this respect, Deleuze and Guattari help our understanding of repression as nothing but a projection of desire: rather than the manifestation of a structure, desire is the possibility of creating thousands of structures. Desire can crystallize structures and turn them into obsessive refrains. Desire constructs traps to entrap desire.

Yet the analytical dispositif forged by Foucault's genealogy and Deleuze and Guattari's creationism predominantly views subjectivity as being capable of causing the desire that was removed to re-emerge in the face of repressive social sublimation; this is an anti-repressive, or, rather, expressive view.

The relationship between structure and desire is the key to the move of Guattari's schizoanalysis outside the orbit of Lacanian Freudianism. For Guattari, desire can be understood neither from the standpoint of structure, nor as a possible variant that depends on the invariance of the mathème; creative desire produces infinite structures, amongst which are also those functioning as dispositifs of repression.

The domain of semio-capital

If we want to leave the Freudian framework behind, we have to approach the position of Jean Baudrillard, whose contribution initially looked like a form of dissuasive thinking. Baudrillard draws a different scenario: in the early 1970s (in *The System of Objects*, *The Consumer Society*, and *Forget Foucault*), he claims that the motor of capitalist development is desire, and the ideology of liberation corresponds to the full domination of the commodity: rather than repression, simulation and the proliferation of simulacra and seduction are the new framework of the imaginary. Baudrillard sees an excess of expressivity as the essential core of this overdose of reality.

The real grows like a desert. Illusions, dreams, passions, madness, drugs, but also the artifice and the simulacrum, all used to
be natural predators of reality. But they've all lost their energy,
as if hit by an incurable and insidious disease (2006: 21).

Baudrillard foresaw a tendency that would become predominant in
the following decades. His analysis shows how simulation transforms the
subject-object relation forcing the subject into the subaltern position of
someone who succumbs to seduction. Rather than the subject, the object
is the agent and the whole question of alienation, repression and the
uneasiness they produce thus fades away.

In the much cited 'Postscript on control societies,' which he wrote
during the last years of his life, Deleuze appears to put under question
the architecture deriving from Foucault's notion of discipline and to move
in the direction of the Baudrillard of the early 1970s. Here, I am not
interested in a comparison between a theory of simulacra and a theory
of desire – which sooner or later deserves to be carried out – but in the
scenario of psychopathologies that emerges as industrial society nears its
end giving way to semiocapitalism, namely, a capitalism founded on
immaterial labor and the explosion of the info-sphere.

Overproduction is an inherent feature of capitalism because, rather
than to the logic of the concrete needs of human beings, commodity production responds to the abstract logic of value production. However, the
kind of overproduction manifest in semiocapitalism is specifically semiotic; an infinite excess of signs circulates in the info-sphere and saturates
individual and collective attention.

Baudrillard's intuition proved to be crucial in the long run. The prevailing pathology of times to come is a product of the generalized com-
pulsion to expression, rather than repression. The first video-electronic
generation shows signs of the effects of pathologies of hyper-expression,
not of repression.

When dealing with the suffering of our times and the discomfort of
the first connective generation, we are no longer in the conceptual framework of Freud's *Civilization and its Discontents*. In Freudianism, at the basis
of pathology lies concealment: something is hidden from us, removed,
and then disappears; we are prevented from something. Evidently, the
basis of pathology today is no longer concealment but hypervision, an
excess of visibility, the explosion of the info-sphere and an overload of
info-neural stimuli.

Not repression, but hyper-expressivity is the technological and anthropological domain of our understanding of the genesis of contemporary psychopathologies such as ADHD, dyslexia, and panic. These indicate a different way of processing informational input, whilst manifesting themselves as suffering, uneasiness and marginalization. Though it might not be necessary, it is worth pointing out that my approach has nothing to do with reactionary and bigot preaching on the evils caused by so-called permissiveness or how good the repression of yesteryear was for our minds and customs.

Pathologies of expressivity

In their introduction to a book on contemporary forms of psychopathology, the editors of *Civiltà e Disagio* [Civilization and discomfort] state:

> Our purpose in this book is to rethink the binomial relationship between civilization and discomfort in the light of the deep social transformations our lives have undergone. One of the most significant of these is a change of sign in the imperative of the social Super-Ego of our times. Whilst the Freudian imperative required a renunciation of instincts, the new social imperative thrusts us towards enjoyment. In fact, the symptoms of discomfort of contemporary civilization are closely related to enjoyment; they are either real practices of it (drug related perversions, bulimia, obesity, and alcoholism), or manifestations of a narcissistic closure that produces stagnations of enjoyment in the body (anorexia, depression, and panic) (Cosenza, Recalcati, Villa: 2006).

Freud identified the dominant social psychopathology with neurosis, which he believed to be the effect of a process of removal; today this is psychosis, which is increasingly associated with the domain of excesses of energy and information, rather than with removal.

In his schizoanalytical works, Guattari concentrated on the possibility of reworking the whole field of psychoanalysis starting from a redefinition of the relationship between neurosis and psychosis, and from the central methodological and cognitive role of schizophrenia. The political effects of his redefinition were very powerful and coincided with the explosion of the neurotic limits imposed on expression by capitalism through the restriction of agency to the repressive boundaries of labor and the subjection of desire to a disciplinary removal; but the very schizo-morphous pressure of movements and the eruption of expression in the social lead to a metamorphosis (or a schizo-metamorphosis) of languages, forms of production and, lastly, capitalist exploitation.

The psychopathologies spreading to the everyday lives of the first generations of the age of connection cannot be comprehended within the repressive and disciplinary framework. Rather than pathologies of removal, they are pathologies of the 'Just do it':

> [H]ence, the centrality of psychosis. Unlike clinical neurosis, which is symbolic because operative within the linguistic and rhetorical domain of removal and the normative foundations of Oedipus, psychosis is always a clinic of the real, not governed by symbolic castration, and thus closer to the truth of structure (it is structurally impossible to symbolize the real of enjoyment as a whole) (Cosenza, Recalcati, Villa, 2006: 4).

The dispersal of identity points to the absence of a center for the identification that occurs in neurosis, which would enable the subject to structure a strong Ego within certain boundaries and become integrated in primary relations with objects and their identification (Cosenza, Recalcati, Villa, 2006: 22).

From the standpoint of semio-pathology, schizophrenia could be seen as an excess of semiotic flows with respect to the power of interpretation. As the universe starts moving too fast and too many signs are calling for our interpretation, the mind is no longer able to distinguish the lines and points that shape things. So we try to grasp meaning through a process of over-inclusion and an extension of the boundaries of signification. In the conclusion to their last joint work, Deleuze and Guattari write:

> We require just a little order to protect us from chaos. Nothing is more distressing than a thought that escapes itself, than ideas that fly off, that disappear hardly formed, already eroded by for-getfulness or precipitated into others that we no longer master. These are infinite *variabilities*, the appearing and disappearing of which coincide. They are infinite speeds that blend into the immobility of the colorless and silent nothingness they traverse, without nature or thought (1994: 201).

Semiotics of schizophrenia

A semiotic regime is repressive when one, and only one, signified is ascribed to each signifier. Whoever fails to interpret the signs of power in the right way, doesn't wave at the flag or respect their superiors, and breaks the law, is in trouble. However, the semiotic regime we find ourselves in as inhabitants of the semiocapitalist universe is characterized by an excess of speed of the signifiers and stimulates a sort of interpretative hyperkinesis. The typical over-inclusion of schizophrenic interpretation becomes the predominant mode of navigation in the proliferating universe of video-electronic media.

In a chapter entitled 'Toward a theory of schizophrenia,' Bateson defined schizophrenic interpretation thus:

> The schizophrenic shows weakness in three fields of the communicative function: a) a difficulty in ascribing the correct mode of communication to messages coming from other people; b) a difficulty in ascribing the correct mode of communication to verbal and non verbal messages; and c) a difficulty in ascribing the right mode of communication to her own thought, sensation and perception (1972: 240).

In the video-electronic info-sphere we all inhabit the conditions that describe schizophrenic communication. Exposed to an overloading of signifying impulses, the human receiver is unable to process the meaning of statements and stimuli in sequence and faces the difficulties listed by Bateson. A further peculiar character of the schizophrenic Bateson mentions is that she does not know how to distinguish metaphor from literary expression.

> The peculiarity of the schizophrenic is not that she uses metaphors, but that she uses them without identifying them (1972: 248).

In the domain of digital simulation, metaphors and things become less and less distinguishable; thing turns into metaphor and metaphor into thing, representation replaces life, and so too life representation. Semiotic flows and commodity circulation juxtapose their codes and become part of the same constellation, which Baudrillard calls hyperreality. Thus the register of schizophrenia becomes the main mode of interpretation. The system of collective cognition loses its critical competence; this amounted to the ability to discern truth value in the statements that were submitted in sequences to relatively alert attention. Amidst the proliferation of fast media, interpretation no longer unfolds along sequential lines; instead, it follows associative spirals and asignifying connections.

Interpretation and overload

In 'Learner based listening and technological authenticity,' Richard Robin, a researcher from George Washington University, studies the effect of the acceleration of speech on listening comprehension. Robin's research is based on a calculation of the number of syllables spoken each second. A faster rate, and more syllables per second decrease the level of the listener's comprehension of meaning: the faster the flow of syllables per second, the less the time for the listener to critically process the message. The speed of emission and the amount of semiotic impulses sent in a given time unit are functional to the time available to a conscious processing.

> Fast speech intimidates listeners. Evidence suggests that global-
> ization has produced faster speech emission rates in areas of the
> world where the Western mode of transmission of signs has come
> to replace traditional and authoritarian ones. For instance, in
> the ex-Soviet Union the speed of transmission measured in syl-
> lables per second has almost doubled since the fall of the com-
> munist regime: from three to almost six syllables per second;
> similar findings reached the same conclusions in the Middle East
> and China (1991: 403).

The implications of Robin's study are extremely interesting for our understanding of the transition from a form of authoritarian biopolitical power that is persuasive (like the totalitarian regimes of the twentieth century) to a form of biopolitical power that is pervasive (like contemporary infocracy).

Persuasive power is founded on consensus: citizens must understand the reasons of the President, General, Secretary or Duce. Only one source of information is authorized. Dissident voices are subjected to censorship. Instead, the infocratic regime of semio-capital grounds its power on overload, the acceleration of semiotic flows and the proliferation of sources of information to the point of the producing the white noise of indistinctiveness, irrelevance and indecipherability. Twentieth century art was conceived as flows of desire and liberating expressions; Surrealism celebrated the expressive power of the subconscious as liberating social and psychic energies. Today, art is also the flow of therapy for mind ecology. Art has replaced the police in the universal dispositif of mind control, but at the same time it looks for inroads into therapy.

Whilst the prevailing epidemic pathology of modernity was the neurosis produced by repression, the pathologies spreading epidemically today manifest signs of psychosis and panic. A hyper-stimulation of attention reduces the ability to critically and sequentially interpret the speech of the other who tries and yet fails to be understood.

The Depression Epidemics

On the morning of April 20th, 2007, I was reading *Il Corriere della sera*.

On the upper corner of page 20, there was a report about the exploits of Cho Seung Hui, the Korean boy who went to look for his girlfriend at Virginia Tech and, not having found her, shot about 30 students and professors at the school.

Weapons, Death, Delirium
The Killer's Video on TV

That was the title of the article: in the picture next to it we saw the boy holding two guns, arms spread apart like in a famous advertisement for Lara Croft's video games.

Up to now, nothing unusual. All the newspapers on the planet had been talking about Cho Seung Hui that day. After having killed two people at 8:30, and before going back to Virginia Tech to kill many more, he had gone home, prepared a package containing a video-testament and sent it to the NBC network which, of course, decided to air it.

But what really got my attention was the image at the bottom of page 20. Initially, after having quickly glanced at it, I thought that it was part of the same story.

Against a black background, I saw the image of a woman with Asiatic, actually Korean, features. She was wearing dark sunglasses, which gave her a stark, aggressive, proud look, and she was portrayed in three different and overlapping poses. In the middle one she is represented frontally while rotating her torso and projecting her head forward and her left arm backward, as if she was launching straight towards you. On the right, the same person is raising one leg and lifting a briefcase made of white synthetic fabric just like her suit. On the left, the position becomes decidedly violent: we see the lady violently kicking an invisible target with her left leg, while her folded right arm seems to be collecting all her available strength.

This was an advertisement for Intel Corp., promoting the new Intel Core 2 Duo processor. And in fact, in the same image, you could read a slogan proclaiming:

INCREASE YOUR FREEDOM
Multiply your performance with the Intel Core 2 processor

Why did they choose a woman to perform in those poses? The Far East transmits aggressive vibrations, indefatigable work ethics, activity, permanent personal mobilization, success in international competitions.

Cho and the advertising team at Intel share the same social imaginary. And the message coming out of the young man's recorded images was the same as the one communicated by the advertisers to their readers.

The panic-depressive cycle

Deadly suicidal explosions are often associated with a pathological diagnosis of depression. There have been many denunciations of the violent suicidal and/or homicidal effects in patients cured with antidepressants which, rather than dealing with the deep psychological implications of depression, simply remove the inhibition to act.

Depression cannot explain Cho's explosion of violence.

Cho's act was complex, creatively conceived and articulated. It was a work of art saturated with symbolic referents taken from contemporary terror-pop. Against a depressive background, confirmed also by the text written by Cho, we see emerging a powerful reaction, aided by easily available substances: psychotropic drugs, terror-pop imagery, precise and powerful weapons. I don't know what kind of substances Cho might have been taking.

That page of the *Corriere della Sera* suggested, by the casual nature of its advertisements, an interpretive key that is irreducible to a depression diagnosis: Cho's violent act is tied to a saturation of emotional circuits, a short circuit caused by overload. This explosively violent behavior follows the loss of control over the relation between informational stimuli and emotional elaboration.

This murderous *acting out* can be the consequence of a depression treated with anti-inhibitory drugs that have no effect on the cause of depression. A whole semiotic universe has grafted itself onto this pharmacological disinhibition, a cascade of semio-stimuli that have brought the organism to an incontrollable hyperexcitation.

The object of study is the panic-depressive cycle.

The message of the Intel corporation, like the whole flux of advertising stimuli, mobilizes a competitive aggression, the violent transgression of rules, the impulsive affirmation of one's own expressivity. The multitasking staged by Intel is the most powerful factor in the intensification of productivity typical of cognitive labor. But multitasking is also a destructuring factor in our faculty to process information rationally, and it overexcites our emotional system in a pathological manner. In the new speech of semiocapitalist hyper-neoliberalism the expression 'Multiply your freedom' actually means 'Multiply your productivity.'

It should be no surprise that the exposure to the informational-advertising-productive stimulating flux produces panic-like, neurasthenic effects, and a pathological irritability. But the succession between mobilizing stimulation of nervous energy and violent action is not linear, because if that were the case all workers undergoing an intense nervous exploitation would become murderers, and this is still not happening. The circuit is more complicated than that. The constant mobilization of nervous energies can lead to a depressive reaction: the frustration of our attempts to act and compete leads the subject to withdraw his or her libidinal energy from the social arena. Our frustrated narcissism retreats and our energy just shuts itself off.

The therapeutic action, at this point, does not address the deep cause of depression, because, as we shall see, this cause cannot be attacked by a pharmacological therapy. The therapeutic treatment of depression implies a deep and extended work of linguistic elaboration, while a pharmacological treatment can act effectively only on the inhibiting blockages, not on the mental causes of depression. And this deblocking action can stimulate a violent action characterized by a depressive background.

Intensification of nervous stimuli, retreat of libidinal investment, painful understanding of narcissism: these are the main aspects of a very widely spread pathological profile in today's society. We can clearly distinguish the pathologies caused by overload (panic, attention disorders, dyslexia) from the ones caused by disinvestment (depression and even autism). But this conceptual distinction should be followed by the recognition that these pathologies, whose origins are different, act simultaneously and complementarily, causing extremely violent manifestations.

Of course, the drugs that remove the inhibitions to act without touching on the depressive core can end up unleashing reckless acts, pure and simple explosions of self-destructive or violent forces.

> After 1980, anxiety neuroses have been divided in two categories: the panic attack and general anxiety syndrome. These two pathologies have quickly migrated in the depressive field, because they can be better treated by antidepressants than with anxiety-reducing medications. Today, anxiety is part of the depressive field. (Ehrenberg 1998: 25).

The basic pathogenic picture emerging from the era of the first connective generation is characterized by the hypermobilizing of nervous energies, by informational overload, by a constant straining of our attention faculties. A particular aspect and an important consequence of this nervous hyper-mobilization is the rarity of bodily contact, the physical and psychical solitude of the info-spheric individual. Within this condition, we have to study depression as a secondary epidemic phenomenon, perfectly integrated in the psychotic-panic etiology of the first connective generation.

Conceptually, I find it interesting to distinguish between depressive and anxiety syndromes, because in the first I see the effect of a stimuli overload, while the second are caused by a disinvestment of energy. But if we want to explain the epidemic explosion of violence at the dawn of our new millennium we have to recognize their connection. A frustrated hyper-excitement leads to a disinvestment of libidinal energy that we call depression. But the subject can explode the depressive block with psychotropic drugs or potentially deadly behavioral shocks.

Sense, depression, truth

Depression can't be reduced to the psychological field. It questions the very foundation of being. Melancholic depression can be understood in relation to the circulation of sense. Faced with the abyss of non-sense, friends talk to friends, and together they build a bridge over the abyss.

Depression questions the reliability of this bridge. Depression doesn't see the bridge. It falls off its radar. Or maybe it sees that the bridge does not exist. Depression doesn't trust friendship, or doesn't recognize it. This is why it cannot perceive sense, because there is no sense if not in a shared space.

Sense is the projection of an intellectual and emotional investment. We can say that sense is the effect of a libidinal investment in interpretation, in the construction of meaning.

The last book by Gilles Deleuze and Félix Guattari, *What is Philosophy?*, contains reflections on old age, friendship, chaos and speed. The theme of depression (always repressed or even denied elsewhere in their work) finally emerges.

> Chaos is defined not so much by its disorder as by the infinite speed with which every form taking shape in it vanishes. It is a void that is not a nothingness but a virtual, containing all possible particles and drawing out all possible forms, which spring up only to disappear immediately, without consistency or reference, without consequence. Chaos is an infinite speed of birth and disappearance. (1994: 118)

And they add:

> Nothing is more distressing than a thought that escapes itself, than ideas that fly off, that disappear hardly formed, already eroded by forgetfulness or precipitated into others that we no longer master. These are infinite variabilities, the appearing and disappearing of which coincide. They are infinite speeds that blend into the immobility of the colorless... (1994: 201)

The infinite acceleration of the world with respect to the mind is the feeling of being definitively cut out from the sense of the world. And immediately it reverses itself, forgetting that kind of feeling that is sense.

Sense is not to be found in the world, but in what we are able to create. What circulates in the sphere of friendship, of love, of social solidarity is what allows us to find sense. Depression can be defined as a lack of sense, as an inability to find sense through action, through communication, through life. The inability to find sense is first of all the inability to create it.

Let's think of a depression caused by love. The lover structures the creation of sense around the person who's the object of his or her desire. The object of love is the magnet attracting the desiring energy. If this object disappears, the ability to create sense is annihilated, and consequently nothing makes sense anymore. "Nothing makes sense to me," says the abandoned lover, and this sentence has a very concrete, not a metaphoric, meaning.

Julia Kristeva, in her *Black Sun*, writes:

> The depressive mood is constituted as a negative narcissistic support, which is nonetheless capable of offering to the ego a certain integrity, although non-verbal. Consequently, the depressive affect acts as a supplement to the non-validation and the symbolic interruption, to the 'it makes no sense' of the depressed subject, while protecting him from the suicidal act. This protection, though, is fragile. The Verleugnung, the depressive denial which annihilates the sense of the symbolic, also annihilates the sense of the act, and it leads the subject to commit suicide without the fear of disintegration, as a rejoining with the archaic non-integration, as lethal as it is jubilatory, oceanic (1988: 24)

If we consider depression the suspension of the sharing of time, as an awakening to a senseless world, then we have to admit that, philosophically speaking, depression is simply the moment that comes closest to truth.

The depressed subject doesn't lose at all the faculty to rationally elaborate the content of his life and of his knowledge: on the contrary, his or her vision can reach an absolutely radical understanding. Depression allows us to see what we normally hide from ourselves through the continuous circulation of a reassuring collective narrative. Depression sees what public discourse hides. Depression is the best condition to access the void that is the ultimate truth.

At the same time, though, depression paralyzes any ability to act, to communicate, to share. It is precisely on this inhibition to act, which is psychically secondary and pragmatically decisive, that the anti-depressants have their effect.

I don't intend to deny that drugs can be effective in treating the symptoms of depression, nor even that by removing the symptoms we can put back into motion a temporarily paralyzed energy, thereby overcoming the very core of the depression. But I want to emphasize the fact that depression is different from its symptoms, and that the cure for depression can follow no other course than the taking care of the impermanent singularity (or of the impermanence of the singular).

The social context of depression epidemics

In his book *La fatigue d'être soi*, Ehrenberg starts from the idea that depression is a disturbance that has to be understood within a social context. In today's highly competitive environment, the depressive syndrome produces an infernal spiral. Depression is caused by a wound to our narcissistic tendencies, and this wound reduces the libidinal energy that we invest in our actions. Consequently, depression is reinforced because it produces a diminution of our activity level and of our ability to compete.

> Depression triumphs when the disciplinary model of behavioral management, the rules concerning authority and conformity typical of a time when interdictions assigned their destiny to the different social classes have retreated in favor of norms that encourage everyone to individual achievement, ordering people to become themselves. The consequence of this new normativity is that the entire responsibility for our lives is located not only in ourselves, but also in the collective space. Depression is an illness of responsibility, dominated by a feeling of inadequacy. The depressed subject is not capable, he is tired of being him or herself (1998: 10)

It is not surprising that depression is spreading at a time when an entrepreneurial and competitive ideology is becoming dominant. Since the beginning of the 1980s, after the defeat of the working class movements and the affirmation of neoliberal ideology, the idea that we should all be entrepreneurs has gained social recognition. Nobody can conceive his or her own life in a more relaxed and egalitarian manner. S/he who relaxes may very well end up in the streets, in the poorhouse or in jail. The so-called neoliberal reforms that are continuously imposed on an increasingly fragmented, defeated, impotent society, which has been crushed by the dominant ideologies, are directed toward the destruction of any economic security for working people, and to expose every worker's life to the risks of the entrepreneurial profession. In the past, taking risks was the job of the capitalist, who invested in his or her own abilities, obtaining enormous gains or suffering painful failures. But economic risk was his business. The others were in a range going from misery to relative prosperity, but they were not encouraged to take risks in order to have more. But today 'we are all capitalist,' as the ideologues of neoliberal reform loudly proclaim, and therefore we all have to take risks. Pensions will no longer given in exchange for the savings accumulated thanks to a life of work, but tied to pension funds that will either produce fabulous revenues or fail miserably, leaving us destitute in our old age. The essential idea is that we all should consider life as an economic venture, as a race where there are winners and losers.

Ehrenberg's analysis sketches the genealogy of the depressive pathologies typical of a generalized entrepreneurial society. A symptomolgical reading of this book, as well as of the 1979 Foucault's book entitled *The Birth of Biopolitics*: Foucault also identifies the spreading of the free enterprise economical model in our ways of living and thinking as the decisive trait of our age. It is the age of neoliberal totalitarianism.

> In corporate life, the disciplinary models typical of Fordism are retreating in favor of norms that push the employees to adopt autonomous behaviors. Participatory management, expression groups, quality circles constitute new ways of enforcing authority, aimed at impressing a spirit of obedience in every salaried worker. These ways of regulating and dominating the workforce are founded on initiative more than on mechanical obedience. A sense of responsibility, the ability to evolve and to create projects, motivation, flexibility: these qualities delineate a new managerial liturgy. The issue is the mobilization of affects and mental capacities much more than dressing the bodies of the salaried workers. The obligations and the ways of defining the problem change: from the mid-1980s on, both work medicine and entrepreneurial sociological research emphasize the new prevalence of anxiety, psychosomatic disorders and depression. Corporate life is the antechamber of depression (Ehrenberg 1998: 199).

In the 1990s, a new pharmacological fashion exploded: substances such as sertraline (Zoloft) and fluorexine (Prozac) flood the market.

Unlike benzodiazepines, a family of drugs which include diazepam (Valium) and bromazepam (Lexotan), these new products don't have a hypnotic, relaxing and anxiety-reducing effect; rather, they have a euphoric effect and make possible the de-blocking of the inhibition to act that constitutes one of the behavioral manifestations of depression.

In the mid-90s, the decade which saw the biggest impulse to the cognitive economy, and that needed the total mobilization of the mental energies necessary for creative labor, there was the birth of a true mythology of Prozac. That product became (and still is) one of the best sellers in pharmacies around the world. The entire managerial class of the global economy went into a constant state of euphoria and psychic alteration. The economical decisions of the global managerial class are a faithful mirror to the substance that allowed the 'deciders' to see only the euphoric aspect of the world, while stubbornly ignoring the devastating effects caused by economic euphoria.

For years, decisions were made with Zoloft impregnated brains or after millions of Prozac tablets had been swallowed. At a certain point, after the financial crisis of Spring 2000 and the political crisis of September 11th, 2001, the world managerial class went into a depressive phase. To cure its own internal void, or maybe to remove the depressing truth of its ethical defeat, the world managerial class has injected itself with a new, dangerous substance: War, an amphetamine that serves to reinvest an aggressivity now destined to destroy the residual energies of the human species and the planet.

The inversion of the future

The future has changed signs, caution Miguel Benasayag and Gérard Schmit in a book entitled *The Age of Sad Passions* (2004), where they reflect on their long therapeutic practice with the youth living in the *banlieues* of Paris. In the modern era, the future was imagined thanks to metaphors of progress. Scientific research and economical entrepreneurship in the centuries of modern development were inspired by the idea the knowledge will lead to an ever more complete mastery of the human universe. The Enlightenment sanctions this conception, and positivism makes of it an absolute belief. The Marxist revolutionary ideologies, guided by a historicist and dialectical vision, also imagined the future on the basis of a progressive teleological model. The present contains, in the form of contradiction, a potential that history is necessarily destined to resolve. It is from the dialectical solution of present contradictions that a social form free from poverty and war will be born. This form is what the Marxist movement calls communism. In the last part of the twentieth century these philosophical premises disintegrated. But what has disappeared, more than anything else, is the credibility of a progressive model for the future.

> The future, the very idea of the future, now bears an opposite sign. Pure positivity becomes negativity, and the promise becomes a threat. Of course, knowledge has developed, but it is unable to suppress human suffering and it feeds the pervading sadness and pessimism (2004: 29)

The future becomes a threat when the collective imagination becomes incapable of seeing possible alternatives to trends leading to devastation, increased poverty and violence. This is precisely our current situation, because capitalism has become a system of techno-economic automatisms that politics cannot evade. The paralysis of the will (the impossibility of politics) is the historical context of today's depression epidemic.

NOTES

1. Translator's note: The title Freud initially chose for this essay was *Das Unglück der Kultur*, which he later changed into *Das Unbehagen in der Kultur*. Whilst Unglück can be translated as 'unhappiness.' Unbehagen would best translate as 'uneasiness' or 'discomfort,' as it means being uneasy, but conscious about one's discomfort and knowing its inescapability; sitting on the edge with arms and hands clasped to one's chest. The term used by the author in Italian is 'disagio,' which expresses a feeling of awkwardness rather than discontent. Given that 'discontent' clearly refers to lack of happiness, which is a notion absent both from the German and the Italian term, 'uneasiness' or 'discomfort' were used.

7. (t)error and Poetry

The century of the future

One hundred years ago Filippo Tommaso Marinetti published the first manifesto of Futurism; the same year, Henry Ford opened his first automobile factory in Detroit. It was the beginning of the century that believed in the future.

The Manifesto asserted the aesthetic value of the machine, that is, the 'external machine,' not to be confused with the internalized and recombining machine of the bio-info era. Futurism exalted the machine as an external object, visible in the city landscape, but now the machine is inside us: we are no longer obsessed with the external machine; instead, the 'info-machine' now intersects with the social nervous system, the 'bio-machine' interacts with the genetic becoming of the human organism.

The Futurist Manifesto declared the aesthetic value of speed. The myth of speed sustained the whole edifice of the imaginary of modernity and acceleration played a crucial role in the history of capital, that is, the history of the acceleration of labor time. Productivity is the growth factor of the accretion of relative surplus value determined by the speed of the productive gesture and the intensification of its rhythm.

Ninety-nine years on since the publication of the Futurist Manifesto, speed has been transferred from the realm of external machines to the information domain. In this process speed became internalized and transformed into a psycho-cognitive automatism. In the century of the future, the machine of speed accomplished the colonization of global space; this was followed by its colonization of the domain of time, lived experience, the mind and perception, which thus sanctioned the beginning of the century with no future.

The question of the relationship between an unlimited expansion of cyberspace and the limits of cyber time, of the time of the mind and of social attention opens up here. At the point of the virtual intersection of the projections generated by countless issuers, cyberspace is unlimited and in a process of continuous expansion. On the contrary, cybertime, that is, the ability of the mind to process information in time, is everything but unlimited: its limits are those of the human mind and are thus organic, emotional and cultural.

Subjected to the infinite acceleration of the info-stimuli, the mind re-acts with either panic or de-sensitization. Sensibility is the faculty that makes empathic understanding possible, the ability to comprehend what words cannot say, the power to interpret a *continuum* of non-discreet elements, non-verbal signs and the flows of empathy. This faculty, which enabled humans to understand ambiguous messages in the context of relationships, might now be disappearing. We are now witness to the development of a generation of human beings lacking competence in sensibility, the ability to empathically understand the other and decode signs that are not codified in a binary system.

Deregulation

Futurism and the Avant-garde set themselves the task of violating rules. Dereglement was the legacy left by Rimbaud to the experimenta-tion of the 1900s. Deregulation was also the rallying cry of the hyper-capitalism of late modernity, paving the way for the development of semio-capital. In the totalitarian period of the external machine and mechanical speed, having previously used the state form to impose its rule on society, capitalism decided to do without state mediation as the techniques of recombination and the absolute speed of electronics made it possible for control to be interiorized.

In the classical form of manufacturing capitalism, price, wages and profit fluctuations were based on the relationship between necessary labor time and the determination of value. Following the introduction of microelectronic technologies and the resulting intellectualization of pro-ductive labor, the relationship between different magnitudes and differ-ent productive forces entered a period of indeterminacy. Deregulation, as launched by Margaret Thatcher and Ronald Regan, marked the end of the law of value and turned its demise into a political economy. In his main work, *Symbolic Exchange and Death*, Jean Baudrillard intuitively in-fers the overall direction of the development of the end of the millennium.

The principle of reality coincided with a certain stage of the law of value. Today, the whole system has precipitated into indeterminacy and reality has been absorbed by the hyper-reality of the code of simulation (1976: 12).

The whole system precipitates into indeterminacy as all correspondences between symbol and referent, simulation and event, value and labor time no longer hold. But isn't this also what the Avant-garde aspired to? Doesn't experimental art wish to sever the link between symbol and referent? In saying this, I am not accusing the Avant-garde of being the cause of liberalist economic deregulation. Rather, I am suggesting that the anarchic utopia of the Avant-garde was actualized and turned into its opposite the moment society internalized rules and capital was able to abdicate both juridical law and political rationality to abandon itself to the seeming anarchy of internalized automatisms, which is actually the most rigid form of totalitarianism.

As industrial discipline dwindled, individuals found themselves in a state of ostensible freedom. No law forced them to put up with duties and dependence. Obligations became internalized and social control was exercized through a voluntary albeit inevitable subjugation to chains of automatisms.

In a regime of aleatory and fluctuating values, precariousness became the generalized form of social relations, which deeply affected the social composition and the psychic, relational and linguistic characters of a new generation as it entered the labor market. Rather than a particular form of productive relations, precariousness is the dark soul of the productive process. An uninterrupted flow of fractal and recombining info-labor circulates in the global web as the agent of universal valorization, yet its value is indeterminable. Connectivity and precariousness are two sides of the same coin: the flow of semiocapitalist production captures and connects cellularized fragments of de-personalized time; capital purchases fractals of human time and recombines them in the web. From the standpoint of capitalist valorization, this flow is uninterrupted and finds its unity in the object produced; however, from the standpoint of cognitive workers the supply of labor is fragmented: fractals of time and pulsating cells of labor are switched on and off in the large control room of global production. Therefore the supply of labor time can be disconnected from the physical and juridical person of the worker. Social labor time becomes an ocean of valorising cells that can be summoned and recombined in accordance with the needs of capital.

Activism

Let us return to the Futurist Manifesto: war and the contempt for women are the essential features of mobilization, which traverses the whole parable of historical vanguards. The Futurist ambition really consisted in mobilising social energies towards the acceleration of the productivity of the social machine.

Art alimented the discourse of advertising as the latter fed into mobilization. When industrial capitalism transposed into the new form of semiocapitalism, it first and foremost mobilized the psychic energy of society to bend it to the drive of competition and cognitive productivity. The new economy of the 1990s was essentially a Prozac-economy, both neuro-mobilization and compulsory creativity.

Paul Virilio has produced important works that show the connection between war and speed: in the modern forms of domination, the imposition of war onto the whole of social life is an implicit one precisely because economic competitiveness is war, and war and the economy share common grounds in speed.

As Walter Benjamin writes: 'all efforts to render politics aesthetic culminate in one thing: war.' The becoming aesthetic of life is one aspect of this mobilization of social energies. The aestheticization of war is functional to the subjugation of everyday life to the rule of history. War forces the global masses to partake in the process of self-realization of the Hegelian Spirit, or, perhaps more realistically, to become part of capitalist global accumulation. Captured in the dynamics of war, everyday life is ready to be subjected to the unlimited rule of the commodity.

From this standpoint, there is no difference between fascism, communism and democracy: art functions as the element of aestheticization and mobilization of everyday life. Total mobilization is terror, and terror is the ideal condition for a full realization of the capitalist plan to mobilize psychic energy. The close relation between Futurism and advertising is an integral part of this process.

In *Art and Revolution* (2007), Gerard Raunig writes on the relationship between the artistic Avant-garde and activism. His work provides a useful phenomenological account of the relation between art and political mobilization in the twentieth century, but it fails to grasp the absolute specificity of the current situation, that is the crisis and exhaustion of all activism.

The term 'activism' became largely influential as a result of the anti-globalization movement, which used it to describe its political communication and the connection between art and communicative action. However, this definition is a mark of its attachment to the past and its inability to free itself from the conceptual frame of reference it inherited from the twentieth century. Should we not free ourselves from the thirst for activism that fed the twentieth century to the point of catastrophe and war? Shouldn't we set ourselves free from the repeated and failed attempt to act for the liberation of human energies from the rule of capital? Isn't the path towards the autonomy of the social from economic and military mobilization only possible through a withdrawal into inactivity, silence, and passive sabotage?

Lenin's depression

I believe that there is a profound relationship between the drive to activism and the male depression of late modernity, which is most evident in the voluntaristic and subjectivist organization of Leninism.

Both from the standpoint of the history of the workers' movement in the 1900s and from that of the strategic autonomy of society from capital, I am convinced that the twentieth century would have been a better century had Lenin not existed. Lenin's vision interprets a deep trend in the configuration of the psyche of modern masculinity. Male narcissism was confronted with the infinite power of capital and emerged from it frustrated, humiliated, and depressed. It seems to me that Lenin's depression is a crucial element for understanding the role his thought played in the development of the politics of late modernity.

I have read Hélène Carrère D'Encausse's biography of Lenin. The author is a researcher of Georgian descent, who in the 1980s also published *L'empire en miettes*, where she foresaw the collapse of the Soviet empire as an effect of the insurgence of Islamic fundamentalism.

What interested me in Carrère D'Encausse's biography of Lenin more than the history of Lenin's political activity was his personal life, his fragile psyche, and his affectionate and intellectual relationships with the women close to him: his mother, his sister, Krupskaia, comrade and wife, who looked after him at times of acute psychological crises, and, finally, Ines Armand, the perturbing, the uneimlich, the lover whom Lenin decided to neutralize and remove, like music, apparently.

The framework of the psyche described in this biography is depression and Lenin's most acute crises coincided with important political shifts in the revolutionary movement. As Carrère D'Encausse writes:

Lenin used to invest everything he did with perseverance, tenaciousness and an exceptional concentration: such consistency, which he thought necessary in each of his efforts, put him in a position of great superiority over the people around him... This feature of his character often had negative effects. Exceedingly intensive efforts would tire him and wear down his already fragile nervous system. The first crisis dates back to 1902 (1998: 78).

These were the years of the Bolshevik turn, of *What is to be done?* Krupskaia played a fundamental role in the crisis of her comrade: she intervened to filter his relations with the outside world, paid for his therapy and isolation in clinics in Switzerland and Finland. Lenin emerged from the 1902 crisis by writing *What is to be done* and engaging in the construction of a 'nucleus of steel,' a block of will capable of breaking the weakest link in the imperialist chain. The second crisis arrived in 1914 at the height of the break up of the Second International and the split of the Communists. The third crisis, as you might guess, occurred in the spring of 1917. Krupskaia found a safe resort in Finland, where Lenin conceived The April Theses and the decision to impose will on intelligence: a rupture that disregarded the deep dynamics of class struggle and forced onto them an external design. Intelligence is depressive, therefore will is the only cure to the abyss, to ignore it without removing it. The abyss remains and the following years uncovered it, as the century precipitated into it.

Here I do not intend to discuss the politics of Lenin's fundamental choices. I am interested in pointing out a relationship between Bolshevik voluntarism and the male inability to accept depression and develop it from within. Here lies the root of the subjectivist voluntarism that produced the setback of social autonomy in the 1900s. The intellectual decisions of Leninism were so powerful because they were capable of interpreting the male obsession with voluntarism as it faced depression.

The next wave

By the beginning of the twenty first century the long history of the artistic Avant-garde was over. Beginning with Wagner's Gesamtkunstwerk and resulting in the Dadaist cry to 'Abolish art, abolish everyday life, abolish the separation between art and everyday life,' the history of the Avant-garde culminates in the gesture of 9/11. Stockhausen had the courage to say this, whilst many of us were thinking the same: terrorising suicide is the total work of art of the century with no future. The fusion of art and life (or death, what difference does it make?) is clearly visible in the form of action that we might call 'terrorizing suicide.' Let us take Pekka Auvinen as an example. The Finnish youngster turned up to his class at school with a machine gun, killing eight people, himself included.

Printed on his T-shirt was the sentence: 'Humanity is overrated.' Wasn't his gesture pregnant with signs typical of the communicative action of the arts?

Let me explain: I am not inviting the young readers of this essay to go to a crowded place with an explosive belt. I am trying to say, pay attention: a gigantic wave of desperation could soon turn into a suicidal epidemic that will turn the first connective generation into a devastating psychic bomb.

I do not think that this wave of suicides can be explained in terms of morality, family values and the weak discourse used by conservative thought to account for the ethical drift produced by capitalism. To understand the contemporary form of ethical shipwreck we need to reflect on the transformations of activity and labor, the subsumption of the time of the mind under the competitive realm of productivity; we have to understand the mutation of the cognitive and psycho-social system.

Conjunction/connection

The context of my understanding of the present historical and cultural dynamics is the transition from a realm of conjunction to one of connection, with a special focus on the emergence of the first connective generation, those who learn more words from a machine than a mother.

In this transition, a mutation of the conscious organism is taking place: to render this organism compatible with a connective environment, our cognitive system needs to be reformatted. This appears to generate a dulling of the faculties of conjunction that had hitherto characterized the human condition.

The realm of sensibility is involved in this ongoing process of cognitive reformatting; we see aesthetic thought as being inserted at a juncture. Ethical and political thought is also reshaping its observational standpoint and framework around the passage from a conjunctive to a connective form of human concatenation.

Conjunction is becoming-other. In contrast, in connection each element remains distinct and interacts only functionally.

Singularities change when they conjoin; they become something other than they were before their conjunction. Love changes the lover and a combination of asignifying signs gives rise to the emergence of a meaning that does not exist prior to it.

Rather than a fusion of segments, connection entails a simple effect of machinic functionality. In order to connect, segments must be compatible and open to interfacing and interoperability. Connection requires these segments to be linguistically compatible. In fact the digital web spreads and expands by progressively reducing more and more elements to a format, a standard and a code that make different segments compatible.

The segments that enter this rhizome belong to different realms of nature: they are electronic, semiotic, machinic, biological, and psychic; optic fibre circuits, mathematical abstractions, electromagnetic waves, human eyes, neurons and synapses. The process whereby they become compatible traverses heterogeneous fields of being and folds them onto a principle of connectivity.

The present mutation occurs in this transition from conjunction to connection, a paradigm of exchange between conscious organisms. Central to this mutation is the insertion of the electronic into the organic, the proliferation of artificial devices in the organic universe, in the body, in communication and in society. Therefore, the relationship between consciousness and sensibility is transformed and the exchange of signs undergoes a process of increasing desensitization.

Conjunction is the meeting and fusion of rounded and irregular forms that infuse in a manner that is imprecise, unrepeatable, imperfect and continuous. Connection is the punctual and repeatable interaction of algorithmic functions, straight lines and points that juxtapose perfectly and are inserted and removed in discrete modes of interaction. These discrete modes make different parts compatible to predetermined standards.

The digitalization of communication processes leads on the one hand to a sort of desensitization to the curve and to the continuous flows of slow becoming, and on the other hand to a becoming sensitive to the code, to sudden changes of states and to the sequence of discrete signs.

Interpretation follows semantic criteria in the realm of conjunction: the meaning of the signs sent by the other as she enters in conjunction with you needs to be understood by tracing the intention, the context, the nuances and the unsaid, if necessary.

The interpretative criteria of the realm of connection on the other hand are purely syntactic. In connection, the interpreter must recognize a sequence and be able to perform the operation required by general syntax or the operating system; there is no room for margins of ambiguity in the exchange of messages, nor can the intention be shown by means of nuances.

This mutation produces painful effects in the conscious organism and we read them through the categories of psychopathology: dyslexia, anxiety and apathy, panic, depression and a sort of suicidal epidemics is spreading.

However, a purely psychopathological account fails to capture the question in its depth, because we are in fact confronted with the effort of the conscious organism to adapt to a changed environment and a readjustment of the cognitive system to the techno-communicative environment. This generates pathologies of the psychic sphere and in social relations.

Aesthetic perception – here properly conceived of as the realm of sensibility and aesthesia – is directly involved in this transformation: in its attempt to efficiently interface with the connective environment, the conscious organism appears to increasingly inhibit what we call sensibility.

By sensibility, we mean the faculty that enables human beings to interpret signs that are not verbal nor can be made so, the ability to understand what cannot be expressed in forms that have a finite syntax. This faculty reveals itself to be useless and even damaging in an integrated connective system. Sensibility slows down processes of interpretation and renders them aleatory and ambiguous, thus reducing the competitive efficiency of the semiotic agent.

The ethical realm where voluntary action is possible also plays an essential role in the reformatting of the cognitive system. Religious sociologists and journalists lament a sort of ethical lack of sensitivity and a general indifference in the behaviour of the new generations. In many cases, they lament the decline of ideological values or community links.

However, in order to understand the discomfort that invests the ethical and political realms, the emphasis needs to be placed on aesthetics. Ethical paralysis and the inability to ethically govern individual and collective life seem to stem from a discomfort in aesthesia – the perception of the other and of the self.

Dystopian poetry

The arts of the 1900s favoured the register of utopia in two forms: the radical utopia of Majakovski and the functional utopia of the Bauhaus. The dystopian thread remained hidden in the folds of the artistic and literary imagination, in Fritz Lang, expressionism, and a kind of bitter surrealism that underlies the field of vision that connects Salvador Dali to Philip Dick. In the second half of the nineteenth century the literary dystopia of Orwell, Burroughs and Delillo flourished. Only today, at the beginning of the twenty first century, does dystopia take center stage and conquers the whole field of the artistic imagination, thus drawing the narrative horizon of the century with no future. In the expression of contemporary poetry, in cinema, video-art and novels, the marks of an epidemic of psychopathology proliferate.

In her videos, Elja Liisa Athila (*Wind*, *If 6 was 9*, *Anne Aki and God*) narrates the psychopathology of relations, the inability to touch and to be touched. In the film *Me and you and everyone we know*, Miranda July tells the story of a video-artist who falls in love with a young man and of the difficulty of translating emotion into words and words into touch. Language is severed from affectivity. Language and sex diverge in everyday life. Sex is talked about everywhere, but sex never speaks. Pills accelerate erection because the time for caresses is limited.

A film by Jia Zhang-Ke, entitled *Still life* (Sanxia haoren) and produced in Hong Kong in 2006, shows an unfolding devastation. This film is extraordinarily beautiful and tells a simple story, with the background of a sad, desolate and devastated China, as both the scenery and its soul. The predominant colour is a rotten, greyish, violet green.

Huo Sanming returns to his place of birth in the hope of finding his wife and daughter, whom he had left years earlier to go and find work in a distant northern mine. His village, along the riverbank of the Yangtze, no longer exists. The construction of the three gorges dam had erased many villages. Houses, people and streets were covered by water. The building of the dam proceeds, the destruction of villages continues and the water is going to keep rising. Huo Sanming arrives in this scenario of devastation and rising water and is unable to find his wife and daughter; so his search begins. He looks for them as groups of workers armed with their picks take walls down, as explosives demolish buildings in the urban center.

After long searches he finally finds his wife, she has aged and been sold by her brother to another man. They meet in the rooms of a building as it is being demolished and talk about their daughter in whispers, with their heads down, against a dark green spaceship background of bricks and iron spattering onto a shit-coloured sky. In the last scene of *Still life*, a tight rope walker walks on a rope from the roofs of a house towards nothingness, against a background that recalls the dark surrealism of Dali's bitter canvas. Still life is a lyrical account of Chinese capitalism, acted inside out, from the standpoint of submerged life.

Corrections, a novel by Jonathan Franzen, speaks of psychopharmacological adjustments as the corrections used by a humanity devastated by depression and anxiety to adjust to an existence that must pretend to be happy. Corrections are the adjustment to a volatile stock market to avoid losing the money invested in private pension funds that might suddenly disappear.

Franzen recounts the old age of a father and mother, a couple of oldies from the Midwest who have gone nuts as a result of decades of hyper-labor and conformism. Corrections are the small and unstoppable slides towards the point of turn-off, the horror of old age in the civilization of competition, the horror of sexuality in the world of puritan efficiency.

Corrections was published in 2001: Franzen digs deep into the folds of the American psyche and describes in minute details the pulpifaction of the American brain, the depression and dementia resulting from a prolonged exposure to the psychic bombardment of stress from work, the apathy, paranoia, puritan hypocrisy and the pharmaceutical industry around them, the psychic unmaking of men who are encapsulated in the claustrophobic shell of economic hyper-protection, the infantilism of a people who pretends to believe, or perhaps really believes in the fulsome

Christmas fairy tale of compassionately liberalist cruelty. By the end of the long awaited Christmas dinner, as the psychopathic family happily gathers together, the father tries to commit suicide by shooting himself in the mouth. He is not successful.

Yakizakana no Uta starts with a fish in cellophane wrapping on a supermarket shelf. A boy grabs it and takes it to the till; he pays, leaves, puts it in the bicycle basket and cycles home.

'Good morning Mr Student, I'm very happy to be with you. Do not worry, I'm not a fish who complains,' the fish says whilst the student briskly pedals home. 'It's nice to make the acquaintance of a human being. You are extraordinary beings; you are almost the masters of the universe. Unfortunately you are not always peaceful, I would like to live in a peaceful world where everyone loves one another and even fish and humans shake hands. Oh it's so nice to see the sunset, I like it ever so much,' the fish becomes emotional and jumps in the cellophane bag inside the basket.

'I can hear the sound of a stream … I love the sound of streams, it reminds me something from my childhood.'

When they get home the boy unpacks the fish and puts it on a plate, throws a little salt on it, as the fish gets excited and says 'Ah! I like salt very much, it reminds me of something …' the boy puts it on the grill in the oven and turns the knob.

The fish keeps chatting: 'Oh Mr Student it's nice here, I can see a light down there … I feel hot … hot …' until its voice becomes hesitant. It starts singing a song, more and more feebly and unconnectedly, like Al in the Space Odyssey as his wires are unplugged.

Yakizakana no Uta, by Yusuke Sakamoto, is perhaps the most harrowing animation film I saw in June 2006 at the Caixa Forum of Barcelona, during the Historias animadas festival. Yet I perceived a common tone running through all of the works presented at the festival, one of ironic cynicism, if you allow me this expression. *Place in time* by Miguel Soares recounts millions of years from the standpoint of an improbable bug, an organic insect, as the world changes around it. *Animales de compania* by Ruth Gomes uses ferocious images to tell the story of a generation of well dressed anthropophagi, young beasts in ties; they run and run to avoid being caught by fellows, colleagues, friends, and lovers who wound, kill and eat them as soon as they fall into their grip, with terrorized smiles and dilated eyes.

This art is no denunciation. The terms 'denunciation' and 'engagement' no longer have meaning when you are a fish getting ready to be cooked.

The art of the twenty first century no longer has that kind of energy, even though it keeps using expressions from the 1900s, perhaps out of modesty, perhaps because it is scared of its own truth. Artists no longer search the way to a rupture, and how could they? They seek a path that leads to a state of equilibrium between irony and cynicism that allows them to suspend the execution, at least for a moment.

Is art the postponement of the holocaust?

All energy has moved to the war front.

Artistic sensibility registers this shift and is incapable of opposing it.

8. Post-Futurism

One hundred years ago, on the front page of *Le Figaro*, for the aesthetic consciousness of the world, Filippo Tommaso Marinetti published the manifesto that inaugurated the century that believed in the future. In 1909 the Manifesto quickly initiated a process where the collective organism of mankind became machinic. This becoming-machine has reached its finale with the concatenations of the global web and it has now been overturned by the collapse of the financial system founded on the futurization of the economy, debt and economic promise. That promise is over. *The era of post-future has began.*

Manifesto of Post-Futurism
Franco "Bifo" Berardi
Creatively read in English by Erik Empson and Arianna Bove

1. We want to sing of the danger of love, the daily creation of a sweet energy that is never dispersed.
2. The essential elements of our poetry will be irony, tenderness and rebellion.
3. Ideology and advertising have exalted the permanent mobilization of the productive and nervous energies of humankind towards profit and war. We want to exalt tenderness, sleep and ecstasy, the frugality of needs and the pleasure of the senses.
4. We declare that the splendor of the world has been enriched by a new beauty: the beauty of autonomy. Each to her own rhythm; nobody must be constrained to march on a uniform pace. Cars have lost their allure of rarity and above all they can no longer perform the task they were conceived for: speed has slowed down. Cars are immobile like stupid slumbering tortoises in the city traffic. Only slowness is fast.
5. We want to sing of the man and the woman who caress one

another to know one another and the world better.

6. The poet must expend herself with warmth and prodigality to increase the power of collective intelligence and reduce the time of wage labor.

7. Beauty exists only in autonomy. No work that fails to express the intelligence of the possible can be a masterpiece. Poetry is a bridge cast over the abyss of nothingness to allow the sharing of different imaginations and to free singularities.

8. We are on the extreme promontory of the centuries... We must look behind to remember the abyss of violence and horror that military aggressiveness and nationalist ignorance is capable of conjuring up at any moment in time. We have lived in the stagnant time of religion for too long. Omnipresent and eternal speed is already behind us, in the Internet, so we can forget its syncopated rhymes and find our singular rhythm.

9. We want to ridicule the idiots who spread the discourse of war: the fanatics of competition, the fanatics of the bearded gods who incite massacres, the fanatics terrorized by the disarming femininity blossoming in all of us.

10. We demand that art turns into a life-changing force. We seek to abolish the separation between poetry and mass communication, to reclaim the power of media from the merchants and return it to the poets and the sages.

11. We will sing of the great crowds who can finally free themselves from the slavery of wage labor and through solidarity revolt against exploitation. We will sing of the infinite web of knowledge and invention, the immaterial technology that frees us from physical hardship. We will sing of the rebellious cognitariat who is in touch with her own body. We will sing to the infinity of the present and abandon the illusion of a future.

Manifesto of Futurism
Le Figarò – February 20th, 1909

1. We intend to sing the love of danger, the habit of energy and fearlessness.

2. Courage, audacity, and revolt will be essential elements of our poetry.

3. Up to now literature has exalted a pensive immobility, ecstasy, and

sleep. We intend to exalt aggressive action, a feverish insomnia, the racer's stride, the mortal leap, the punch and the slap.

4. We affirm that the world's magnificence has been enriched by a new beauty: the beauty of speed. A racing car whose hood is adorned with great pipes, like serpents of explosive breath - a roaring car that seems to ride on grapeshot is more beautiful than the *Victory of Samothrace*.

5. We want to hymn the man at the wheel, who hurls the lance of his spirit across the Earth, along the circle of its orbit.

6. The poet must spend himself with ardor, splendor, and generosity, to swell the enthusiastic fervor of the primordial elements.

7. Except in struggle, there is no more beauty. No work without an aggressive character can be a masterpiece. Poetry must be conceived as a violent attack on unknown forces, to reduce and prostrate them before man.

8. We stand on the last promontory of the centuries! Why should we look back, when what we want is to break down the mysterious doors of the Impossible? Time and Space died yesterday. We already live in the absolute, because we have created eternal, omnipresent speed.

9. We will glorify war – the world's only hygiene – militarism, beautiful ideas worth dying for, and scorn for woman.

10. We will destroy the museums, libraries, academies of every kind, will fight moralism, feminism, every opportunistic or utilitarian cowardice.

11. We will sing of great crowds excited by work, by pleasure, and by riot; we will sing of the multicolored, polyphonic tides of revolution in the modern capitals; we will sing of the vibrant nightly fervor of arsenals and shipyards blazing with violent electric moons; greedy railway stations that devour smoke-plumed serpents; factories hung on clouds by the crooked lines of their smoke; bridges that stride the rivers like giant gymnasts, flashing in the sun with a glitter of knives; adventurous steamers that sniff the horizon; deep-chested locomotives whose wheels paw the tracks like the hooves of enormous steel horses bridled by tubing; and the sleek flight of planes whose propellers chatter in the wind like banners and seem to cheer like an enthusiastic crowd.

Translated by R. W. Flint

Glossary

Automatism

We speak of automatism every time the succession of two states of being (of language, society, and action) appears as one inescapable chain: as one implication of logical type, and as one succession logically determined. In the political history of our time the feeling of finding oneself taken in a chain of automatisms has become progressively stronger. More and more we have the impression that political decision counts for nothing and is limited to faithfully recording and reproducing the lines established by the chain of automatisms incorporated in the social machine. In the modern age, political decision seemed to be able to modify the course of events, opening new perspectives, disrupting and overturning the existing social conditions. Today experience teaches us that this *potenza* of politics has been dissolved. It makes very little difference to the legislative activity, to labor and economic organization, that there are political forces of the right or the left in the government. Economic rule, the abstract dynamics of growth, and the absolute duty of competition prevail as a law that is superior to the human will. Economic automatism is the dogma to which those who want to obtain political power, both right and left coalitions, kowtow. However, the dominant economic dogmatism of the present time is not only a consequence of conformism. The conformism of politicians is an integrating part of it, but it is not the essential element. The essential element is deeply inscribed in the architecture of technological, financial, economic, psychical automatisms that structure the behavior of human agents in an inescapable way.

Cognitariat

In the industrial age the word 'proletariat' designated the social class of those who held no property apart from the *prole* (the sons) and

the strength of their arms. Because of owning no property the proletarians were forced to accept a condition of waged labor, that is a condition of lifetime service and systematic exploitation. In the sphere of
semio-capital, the class of producers is composed mostly of people who
have no property apart from their own cognitive capacity: nervous
energy expressed in form of creativity and language. When cognitive
capacities are set to work, their concrete role and use value (knowing,
expressing, and communicating) are submitted to the economic purpose of increasing capital. Information technologies transform every
process into an exchange of signs, and the cognitarian is one who produces goods through the act of language. This involves the expropria-
tion of what is most intimately human: language. Language is therefore
separated from daily life, from corporeality and affectivity, in order to
become a captive of capital. Cognitive activity is separated from its
social function and its corporeality. This separation constitutes the specific form of alienation of cognitive labor. The cognitariat is 'cognitive
proletariat': social class of those who experiences this separation.

Compatibilization

Every sensitive agent, in order to be productive and operative, must
be compatible with the format that regulates the exchanges and makes
possible the generalized inter-operability in the system. The expansionary
dynamic of the Internet requires that feeling agents all work following
the same format that is translated in the principle of economic competition.

In a system of information exchanges the format acts as an absolutely
crucial, selective and marginalizing factor. If you try to send signals using
a different format from the one used to program the Internet, your signals
will become illegible, incomprehensible, and ineffective. The power of
the Internet has therefore quickly been revealed as a power of a depersonalization system, that is, the annihilation of singularity marks. The
mediatic system has created the conditions for an enlarged reproduction
of a knowledge without thought, of a purely functional, operational, and
lacking of any self-directing dispositive knowledge.

Composition and Compositionism

How does it happen that an ensemble of individuals is able to become
a conscious collective subjectivity? Imaginary flows, world expectations,

ritual habits and mythologies are diffused as they were chemical agents in the psycho-sphere, and this diffusion makes possible the transformation of formless aggregates in conscious collectivities that are able to identify themselves more or less provisionally in a common intentionality. This formative process of the collective resembles much more a chemical composition than the mechanical accumulation of organizational forms. There is an implicit critique of political subjectivism and, at the time same, a critique of empirical sociology within the concept of composition (and re-composition). The social process comes to be understood as a heterogeneous *becoming* where technological segments, cultural sedimentations, political intentions, ideological representations, and mechanical and communicating concatenations intervene, and escape the voluntaristic and mechanical reductionism of politics and sociology.

Cybertime

We call cybertime the mental time that is necessary to elaborate info-stimuli coming from cyberspace. Cyberspace is a space of unlimited expansion by definition, since it is the virtual dimension produced by countless semiotic agents that project their signals in the infinite space of the Internet. The unlimited expansion of cyberspace produces an infinitely higher mass of info-stimuli than the one that can be elaborated by the cybernaut's conscious brain. Since the expansion of cyberspace takes place within the conditions of a market economy, where the supply must meet the demand so that the production of surplus value can be achieved, and the investment of capital can be profitable, the mental time undergoes a continuous pressure: it must in fact receive, decode and consume the increasing mass of info-goods that cyberspace contains. However cybertime is not unlimited. On the contrary, the mental time available to a conscious and sensitive organism is limited by organic factors (sleep, disease, deterioration, attention limits), by cultural factors (beliefs, expectations from the world), and by emotional factors (affectivity, slowness needed for the psychical elaboration of signals). Therefore, the relationship between cyberspace and cybertime create the conditions for a continuous semiotic overproduction, which have psychotic effects on the mind exposed to the cyberspace flow, and the effect of overproduction on the economy.

De-socialization

Time privatization and generalized competitiveness produce a de-socializing effect in conditions of precarity. However this de-socialization does not allow us to enjoy the autonomy of solitude, because we are exposed to an invasive socialization that is always possible and *in ambush*. We are continuously forced to socialize with competitive and hostile alterities: we live in a condition of hyper-socialized de-socialization.

Fractal work

With the term fractal, Benoit Mandelbrot means to define a geometric object that is repeated in its structure on different scales. The word derives from the Latin fractus (divided, broken, to be cracked, that it exactly means breaking). With the expression fractal finance Mandelbrot means the complex financial market dynamics that combine and recombine always increasing masses of fragments of financial capital between them equivalent. Thanks to Internet dynamics it has become possible to continuously combine and recombine fragments of working time. To this extent, fractalization means the fragmentation and the recombination of working time according to different sequences. Thanks to the fractalization and the flexibility of labor, the physical and legal existence of the worker is erased, as he is reduced to an interchanging supplier of fragments of recombinant and semiotic time. Therefore the worker becomes a machine provided with nervous system that can be used for a variable period of time, and that it is paid for the period of occasional and temporary time that it has been employed for. The time of fractal labor can also be defined as cellular because it corresponds to a cell of the fractal ocean of recombinant time that has taken the place of the labor market. Cognitive labor can be considered as an ocean of time fragments, and the cellular technique makes possible the meeting (through the cell phone) and the recombination of these fragments. To this extent, we can consider the cell phone as the assembly line of cognitive labor.

Hyper-labor

The prediction that the development of informatic technologies would determine a reduction of social working time by promoting automation, has been revealed as false. Rather than moving toward a progressive reduction of working time, as André Gorz, Jeremy Rifkin and many other sociologists and futurologists had predicted, we are moving toward a form of hyper-labor without social securities, without legal restrictions, and without any respect for human life. Since the 1980s average labor time has increased in a constant way, and since the beginning of the new century the increase of absolute and relative exploitation has become impressive. The typical employee worked an extra 148 hours in 1996 than his colleague did in 1973. The percentage of people who work more than 49 hours per week has increased from 13% in 1976 to nearly 19% in 1998, according to the US Bureau of Labor Statistics. In addition, the percentage has gone up from 40% to 45% in the case of *managers*. In the course of the twentieth century the main achievement of the workers movement has been the reduction of legal working hours to forty hours weekly and the right of restrictions on overtime. This right has been completely erased in the last decade. Global capitalism employs slave-labor on a wide scale. In the great majority of the countries in the world, legal limitations on exploitation no longer have any value.

Imaginary

With the word imaginary we imply a magmatic and not symbolically ordered accumulation of images and rich of imagery solicitations that the conscious organism receives in the course of its info-spheric exposure.

Info-labor

With the notion of 'abstract labor' Marx defined a process of separation of working activity from its specific and concrete utility and therefore from its particular form of ability: work performance more and more loses its characters of individuality, specificity and concreteness in the process of abstraction, so that it becomes a repetitive act of abstract production of exchange value. The informatization of production processes constitutes a leap in the process of abstraction. Industrial labor consisted in the transformation of mechanical matter by an operator who applied its physical energies in the process of goods production. After the informatization of production techniques, processes of transformation increasingly become processes of elaboration of information. Info-labor is the activity that produces material and immaterial goods through the elaboration of information. The process of social info-labor is innervated by the digital net, that works as a super-organism capable of subsuming and liquefying fragments of abstract, uniformed, and re-combinable human time.

Info-sphere

If cyberspace is the space of interconnection of mental activity between infinite sensitive agents provided with instruments for the transmission and the reception of signs, and it is the sphere of relation between bio-informational organisms, the info-sphere is then the field where semiotic flows circulate from innumerable transmitters to reach innumerable receivers. Cyberspace is the field where conscious organisms are formed as interconnected receptive cells. Info-sphere is the field where meaningful and intentional signs circulate, and it is the conductor field of informative solicitations that stimulate the human terminal. Therefore info-sphere means the field where signs circulate originating from transmitters, and cyberspace emphasizes the character of interaction between sensitive agents that interconnect with each other.

Info-stimulus

We call information the arranged and intentional violation of the entropic order of the universe, that is the recording of a content of communicable knowledge in form of signal, and we call info-stimulus the solicitation that transmitters exercise on the conscious organism to induct its consumption of info-goods. The info-stimulus exercises a pressure on the conscious attention provoking an excitation that can be carried to exhaustion. The signs possess a twofold character: they are immaterial in so far as they are holders of meaning, but they are material in so far as they are stimulators of the nervous system. The sign has a graphical and phonic materiality, and produces material effects from the muscular, affective, nervous point of view. Info-stimulus is therefore the material effect produced on the conscious and sensitive organism by signs that hold information.

Info-time in recombination

In the passage from the systems of traditional machines to the systems of the Internet, the abstraction process involves the very nature of human time, and modifies the subjective perception in the conscious organism. Capital needs no longer to employ a human being in order to deduct the objective time that the person holds. It can take possession of separated fragments of the worker's time in order to recombine them in a separated sphere from his individual life. Therefore an absolute separation occurs between subjective perception of the time that flows and objective recombination of the time in the value production. Capitalists no longer need to buy the entire lifetime of a worker, but it is enough to capture isolated fragments of time, moments of attention and operability. The labor needed in order to make the Internet work is not labor concentrated in one person. It is a constellation of moments that are isolated in space and fractioned in time, recombined in the fluid machine of the Internet. In order to be incorporated by the Internet, fragments of working time must be rendered compatible, and reduced to a single format that makes possible a general inter-operability.

Media activism

Media activism lives a condition of ambiguity: it participates in the process of post-human mutation, but it tries to change the route, to prevent what makes human life worthy and pleasant getting lost in that process, that is, the communication between conscious and sensitive organisms. The task of media activism is neither to oppose the connective mutation in course, nor to govern it. During the course of mutation its task is to maintain alive competences that are cognitive, active, creative, aesthetic, and ethics and whose continuity is threatened.

Media-sphere

This can be defined as the assemblage of semiotic-imaginary transmitters that innervate the info-sphere with their flows.

Neuro-telematic Rhizome

Cyber-space is a world hypothesis where the ontological and the gnoseological dimensions interfere. The world is the totality of the projections of effective and possible mental states (virtual experiences); but the world is also the place of surprise, imagination, experiences not yet tried out, and discovery and creation of new dimensions of an experience not yet actualized. The projective 'mentalism' engages with an impetuous transformation of the atmosphere where man lives, thinks and communicates. This transformation is due to the unlimited diffusion of technical instruments of amplification, reproduction, and simulation. The nervous system is entwined with the infinite lines of reticular connection.

Precarity

Precarious is person who is able to know nothing about one's own future and therefore is hung by the present and praises God to be rescued from the earthly hell (the term precarity derives from praying). We speak of precarious labor when labor is subordinated to a form of flexible and unregulated exploitation, subjected to daily fluctuations of the labor market, and forced to endure the blackmail of a discontinuous salary. The precarious worker is not formally employed, and still his existence is not at all free, the waged relationship is discontinuous and occasional, and still the dependence is continuous and full of anxiety.

In the 1970s and 80s when the dismantling of the Fordist system and guaranteed wages tied to industrial production began, precarious working conditions appeared as a marginal and temporary phenomenon that concerned above all the young workers that entered into the labor market. Today it is clear that labor precariousness is no longer a marginal condition, but it is the black heart of the process of global capitalistic production. Precarization is the consequence of the deterritorialization of all aspects of production. There is no continuity in the work experience: one does not go to the same factory, does not cover the same journey, and does not meet the same people everyday, as it was in the industrial age. Therefore it is not possible to implement forms of permanent social organization. Since labor became precarious thanks to a cellular and reticular transformation, the problem of the autonomous organization of labor must be completely rethought. We still do not know in which way this organization can be constructed: this is the main political problem of the future.

Psycho-sphere

Psycho-sphere is the soft face of info-sphere, it is the field where the recording and the psychical elaboration of the info-stimuli occurs. The consequences of "info-vasion," nervous overload, psychopharmacology penetration, and fractalization of working and existential time, are manifested in the psycho-sphere. The psycho-sphere is the unpredictable effect that info-vasion devices produce in the interconnected global mind. The acceleration and intensification of nervous stimuli on the conscious organism seem to have thinned the cognitive film that we can call sensibility. As the mass of info-stimuli increases, the time available for the elaboration of the nervous stimuli reduces. The conscious organism accelerates the cognitive, gestural, and kinetic reactivity. As a consequence, our empathetic capacity seems to decrease.

Recombination/recombinant

The concept of recombination emerges as a result of the discovery of the DNA in biological and specifically biogenetic fields. Even before manifesting itself on the epistemological level, the concept of recombination circulated in literature from the experimentations of OULIPO to the writings of Raymond Roussel, the *cadavre exquis* of the Surrealists and the novels of Nanni Balestrini. Recombination is a cognitive and operative method that crosses the most dynamic fields of research and action. Passing from the analogical to the digital, the flows of speech, image, and sound perform like the activity of cutting and sewing, of dissembling and assembling to increasingly narrow scales. If we accept the idea that the recombinant principle is the key of post-mechanical technologies, and we assume this principle as an interdisciplinary epistemic paradigm, we will notice that it delineates a common field with the phenomena of life and language. Informatic and biogenetic technologies are constructed upon the logic of recombination, that is a meaningless and not dialectical logic: recognizable forms and meaningful ensembles emerge from pure informational sequences (e.g. zero and one that reveal the image on the computer screen, the four components of the DNA that reveals the living organisms). Deleuze and Guattari say in *Anti-Oedipus*: I don't care at all about my mum and my dad, about Oedipus, or the original trauma and so on. I am interested in knowing how the language dismantles and rearranges reality, I am interested in knowing how to recombine signs and gestures and bodies in order to find a way out, in order to free desire from its labyrinth.

Semio-capitalism

Semiotics is the science that studies signs. We call capitalism a social system founded on the exploitation of labor and finalized to the accumulation of capital. We can talk of semio-capitalism when informational technologies make possible a full integration of linguistic labor with capital valorization. The integration of language in the valorization process obviously involves important consequences both in the economic field and in the linguistic sphere. In fact it is possible to calculate the working time that is necessary to carry out a mechanical operation, but it is not possible to calculate the average working time socially needed to elaborate signs and create new forms in a precise way. Therefore linguistic labor is hardly reducible to the Marxian law of value, and consequently the economy incorporates new factors of instability and indefiniteness once the valorization becomes dependent on language. In turn language incorporates economic rules of competition, shortage, and overproduction. That is how an excess of signs (supply) is generated that cannot be consumed and elaborated in the time of social attention (demand). The consequences of semiotic overproduction are not only economic, but also psychical, since language acts directly on the psycho-sphere.

Sensibility/Sensitivity

Sensibility is the faculty that allows human beings to comprehend psychical contents that are not and they cannot be verbalized. Sensibility constitutes a film that makes the empathetic contact between conscious organisms possible. Sensibility is the faculty that allows us to connect to the co-evolution of parallel-less beings that have nothing to do with each other. In other words, it is the faculty of entering in harmony with the rhizome. If therefore sensibility is the ability to grasp the meaning of what cannot be expressed in words, sensitivity is the ability to feel the skin of the other in a pleasurable way. These two faculties together make possible what Buddhism calls Great Compassion, which is the ability to perceive the body of the other as continuation of one's own body, the possibility of feeling the pleasure of the other as one's own pleasure, and the pain of the other as one's own pain. However, when a gap is created between these two faculties, the disturbance of the epidermic perception of the one becomes the inability to comprehend the meaning of the signs that come from the other. Thus war reigns between men.

Territorialization/Deterritorialization

Territorialization is the effect of acknowledgment by a conscious organism of an imaginary and ritual territory, through an identity code that can manifest itself in ethical values, shared memories, and mythologies. The identity code generally has an excluding effect and makes possible the mobilization of aggressive energies towards the other who does not possess the same code, and therefore does not belong to the territory. Deterritorialization is the disconnection of the conscious organism from its identity code, the effect of non-acknowledgment of the imaginary, psychical and ritual territory. The history of capitalism is history of a continuous process of deterritorialization. However, since the cultural and psychical substratum that constitutes capitalism is an identity substratum, a movement of reterritorialization follows each deterritorialization, that manifests itself through rituals of aggressive re-identification: violence, racism, war.

Bibliography

Bateson, Gregory (2000) *Steps to an ecology of mind*. Chicago: University of Chicago Press.

Baudrillard, Jean (1971) "Requiem pour les media," *Utopie* 4 October 1971: 35-51.

Baudrillard, Jean (1977) "Forgetting Foucault," Trans. Nicole Dufresne, *Humanities in society* 3/1. Winter 1980: 87-111.

Baudrillard, Jean (1993) *Symbolic Exchange and Death*. London: Sage.

Baudrillard, Jean (1996) *The system of objects*. Trans. James Benedict. London: Verso.

Baudrillard, Jean (1997) *The consumer society: myths and structures*. Trans. George Ritzer. London: Sage.

Baudrillard, Jean (2006) *Il Patto di lucidità o l'intelligenza del Male* [The Intelligence of Evil or the Lucidity Pact]. Milan: Raffaello Cortina Editore.

Benasayag, Migel and Gérard Schmidt (2004) *L'epoca delle passioni tristi*. Milano: Feltrinelli.

Carrère D'Encausse, Hélène (1998) *Lenin*. Paris: Fayard. Lenin (2002) Trans. George Holoch, NJ: Holmes & Meier.

Cosenza, Domenico, Massimo Recalcati, and Angelo Villa, Eds. (2006) *Civiltà e disagio. Forme contemporanee della psicopatologia*. Milan: Mondadori.

Deleuze, Gilles (1990) "Postscript on control societies," *Negotiations*. Trans. Martin Joughin. New York: Columbia University Press.

Deleuze, Gilles and Félix Guattari (2000) *Anti-Oedipus. Capitalism and schizophrenia*. Trans. Robert Hurley, Mark Seem and Helen R. Lane. London: Athlone Press.

Deleuze, Gilles and Félix Guattari (1994) *What is philosophy?* Trans. Hugh Tomlinson and Graham Burchill. London: Verso.

Ehrenberg, Alain (1998) *La fatigue d'être soi*. Paris: Odile Jacob

Foucault, Michel (1975) *The birth of the clinic. An archaeology of medical perception*. Trans. Alan Sheridan. New York: Vintage Books.

Foucault, Michel (2006) *History of madness*. Trans. Jonathan Murphy and Jean Khalfa. London: Routledge.

Foucault, Michel (1977) *Discipline and punish. The birth of the prison*. Trans. Alan Sheridan. New York: Vintage Books.

Foucault, Michel (2008) *The Birth of Biopolitics: Lectures at the Collège de France, 1978-1979*. Trans. Ian Hamilton Grant. London: Sage.

Freud, Sigmund (1982) *Civilization and its discontents*. Trans. Joan Riviere. London: Hogart Press.

Gates, Bill (1999) *Business @ the Speed of Thought*. New York: Warner Books.

Heidegger, Martin (1993) *Basic Writings*. Ed. David Farrell Krell London: Routledge.

Jungk, Robert (1958) *Brighter than a Thousand Suns: A Personal History of the Atomic Scientists*. New York: Harcourt Brace.

Krahl, Hans Juergen (1969) *Costituzione e Lotta di Classe*. Milano: Jaka Book.

Kristeva, Julia (1988) *Il sole nero*. Milano: Feltrinelli.

Lovink, Geert (2003) *Dark Fiber: Tracking Critical Internat Culture*. Cambridge: MIT University Press.

Marcuse, Herbert (1987) *Eros and civilization. A philosophical inquiry into Freud*. London: Ark Paperbacks.

Marx, Karl (1973) *Grundrisse*. New York: Penguin.

Neisser, Ulric (1976) *Cognition and Reality: Principles and Implications of Cognitive Psychology*. San Francisco: W. H. Freeman.

Raunig, Gerald (2007) *Art and Revolution: Transversal Activism in the Long Twentieth Century*. Trans. Aileen Derieg. New York: Semiotext(e).

Robin, Richard (1991) "Authentic Russian video: where are we going? Where do we go?" *Slavic and East European Journal* Vol. 35, No.3: 403-410.

Sartre, Jean Paul (1976) *Critique of dialectical reason*. Trans. Alan Sheridan. London: Verso.

Saviano, Roberto (2006) *Gomorrah*. Trans. Virginia Jewiss. New York: Farrar, Straus and Giroux.

Sennett, Richard (1988) *The Corrosion of Character: The Personal Consequences of Work In the New Capitalism*. New York: WW Norton & Company.

Minor Compositions

you can find them at yr local undercommons...
...or better yet,

create your own....

www.minorcompositions.info